GEORGE WASHINGTON
PIONEER FARMER

Alan and Donna Jean Fusonie

Foreword by Nancy Kassebaum Baker

Mount Vernon Ladies' Association
Mount Vernon, Virginia 22121

This publication was made possible by
the family and friends
of the late Mrs. Alexander L. Wiener.

The Mount Vernon Ladies' Association
Mount Vernon, Virginia
©1998 by The Mount Vernon Ladies' Association.
All rights reserved. Published 1998.
Reprinted 2003, 2011

Cover illustration: Claude Regnier after Junius Brutus Stearns,
Life of George Washington/The Farmer. Lithograph, 1853.
Collection of the Mount Vernon Ladies' Association.

ISBN: 0-931917-28-X

To the memory of

Mrs. Alexander L. Wiener
Vice Regent for Michigan (1964-1989)
of the
Mount Vernon Ladies' Association

Foreword

For someone who has long admired our first president from a lawmaker's viewpoint, it has been fascinating to rediscover George Washington as one of our nation's most remarkable farmers. Those who grew up in America's wheat belt can rightfully describe Washington as a kindred spirit.

In his late twenties, Washington made a pivotal decision. He moved away from the typical Chesapeake practice of cultivating tobacco and turned instead to grains. He was not only bucking tradition, he had made up his mind that the future of American farming lay in diversity and utility. You cannot, after all, use tobacco to feed a nation, particularly one growing at such a rapid pace.

Although he spent nearly half his adult life away from his Mount Vernon farms, serving his country as commander in chief and president, Washington always preferred to be wading through his fields of wheat. Was it ready for harvest? He would snatch the head of a plant, rub the kernels between his hands, let the chaff blow away in the breeze. Biting down on the grain – a palpable exercise perfected by years of experience – Washington would feel the give of the shell, taste the moisture of the pulp. If the time was right, he would then summon all his field hands, as well as carpenters, painters and masons, to get the grain in.

Today, only a tiny percentage of American farmland is cultivated by individual owners. We can wax nostalgic for the days when family operations fed our communities, but Washington may not have shared this sentimental approach. He took the long view and he was determined that American farmers place themselves on the cutting edge of technological advances. When Washington grew impatient with ineffective and wasteful threshing practices, he cleared his presidential desk in Philadelphia, moved aside treaties and pending bills, and designed a 16-sided treading barn the likes of which the nation had never seen. It was likely that he worked on his design before breakfast or at the end of an exhausting day.

Innovations and creative techniques applied by Washington at his Potomac estate were showcased for the domestic and foreign visitors who flooded Mount Vernon. One French visitor noted that Washington was "constantly employed in the management of his farm, in improving his lands, and in building barns." Following a tour of Mount Vernon's vast pastureland, Washington proudly explained to his French guests that "it was his intention to set his country the example of cultivating artificial meadows."

Complex crop rotation schemes, a mule-breeding program, experiments with a wide variety of fertilizers – all of these were intended to provide long-term returns to America's farmers. As on the battlefield and in the halls of government, Washington led best by example, not by fiery oratory – his deeds were deafening enough.

As a pragmatist, Washington had little patience for theory. Only, he told a fellow practitioner, "from a course of experiments by intelligent and observant farmers" could American agriculture live up to its early promise. As humble as he was, Washington would not admit to being our nation's "First Farmer," the leader of a movement that would one day fulfill his hope that "some day . . . we shall become a storehouse and granary for the world."

As a Kansan and an American, I am immensely satisfied that our nation's farmers have accepted and more than met Washington's challenge.

SENATOR NANCY KASSEBAUM BAKER
Burdick, Kansas

Preface

This publication provides a fresh historical focus upon George Washington as a pioneer farmer actively engaged in a new approach to agriculture – one based upon a more scientific attitude towards crops, farm animals, and the land. As the authors examined his correspondence and diaries, the emerging profile of George Washington was of a tireless experimenter, eager to share his results with visitors and with farmers in other parts of the country and abroad. In his correspondence, Washington used the power of his pen to convey important agricultural thoughts. He increasingly expressed his concern about the ruinous agricultural practices of many of his fellow farmers. Washington's complex shift to a more self-reliant and integrated system of agriculture reveals him to be an informed, forward-thinking decision maker who focused on the long-term productivity and conservation of his land at Mount Vernon. The authors, also practicing farmers, are intrigued by the similarity between Washington's outlook and that of an increasing number of today's farmers who use more sustainable approaches.

This monograph in no way purports to be either a full-scale account of Washington's agricultural life nor an in-depth comprehensive history of his agricultural interests. Rather, the authors have tried to present an overview of Washington the farmer hoping to stimulate a renewed interest among the readers and writers of agricultural history to explore the possibilities of new research which will portray Washington in a relevant way to new generations of Americans.

The research involved in this publication is based primarily upon the unpublished agricultural notebooks located in the George Washington Papers at the Library of Congress, Washington's published diaries and papers, and a collection of published letters written to one of his farm managers. The following facilities proved invaluable in the research process: the Mount Vernon Reference and Research Library; the Washington Collection of the Boston Athenaeum, which houses the greatest number of books formerly owned by Washington; the Rare Book Collection of the National Agricultural Library, which is particularly strong in 18th-century British and American agriculture; and the unpublished records and library of the Philadelphia Society for Promoting Agriculture located at the University of Pennsylvania. Other libraries containing relevant reference materials include McKeldin Library at the University of Maryland, the Maryland Hall of Records, and the Calvert County Historical Society in Prince Frederick, Maryland. For their constructive advice as well as their full confidence and encouragement, the authors are especially indebted to the following individuals at Mount Vernon: John Riley, Historian; Barbara McMillan, Librarian; and James Rees, Resident Director. Thanks also to the staff at Mount Vernon for their dedication in preserving the historical authenticity of the Mansion and grounds and in providing vivid glimpses into Washington's agricultural life through their educational and interpretive programs.

Most of Washington's writings reveal his tireless sense of responsibility for not only the farming activities and land at Mount Vernon but, just as important, his vision for the nation of farmers. With a renewed interest in George Washington, the farmer, generations of researchers have a unique opportunity to begin an in-depth inquiry into the many fascinating aspects of his agricultural life. As we commemorate the 200th anniversary of Washington's death in 1999, let all Americans, especially the young, take the opportunity to learn more about the character, determination, perseverance, and creativity of this truly amazing American farmer.

An Aspiring Planter

The year 1732 was a significant one, indeed, for a young America. Benjamin Franklin, at age 26, had just published *Poor Richard's Almanac,* a compilation of weather predictions, epigrams, and proverbs. Growing numbers of travelers included the Scotch-Irish immigrant settlers moving out of western Pennsylvania down the Shenandoah Valley into Virginia and farther south. Perhaps they had been inspired by a new travel and guide book, *The Vade Mecum for America: or A Companion for Traders and Travellers,* that had recently been printed. Robert Prince, a farmer in Long Island, New York, began growing plants for his own family garden, which his son later expanded and developed into a successful commercial nursery. This was also the year that George Washington – surveyor, farmer, military leader, and first president of the United States – was born at Pope's Creek in Westmoreland County, Virginia, the first child of Augustine Washington, an up-and-coming planter, and his second wife, Mary Ball. George Washington and myth became inseparable from his earliest days as the story was later told of Augustine Washington planting "seeds which, when they grew, wrote the name of his child – George Washington."

In a colony that based its value on tobacco production, it is not surprising that the first Washington to reach America arrived in 1657 on a ship scheduled to carry the leaf back to England. As it turned out Colonel John Washington, George Washington's great-grandfather, stayed and settled in Westmoreland County. From the beginning, George Washington was destined to be a part of the Virginia tobacco trade, the origin and development of which embraced a long sweep of earlier history and traditions tied to the cultivation of tobacco in North America. Ultimately, with the passage of time, Washington faced the realities of the Virginia tobacco economy and chose a more challenging, diverse, and integrated system of agriculture based upon experimentation, innovation, and entrepreneurship.

The Chesapeake Bay society and economy into which George Washington was born had its roots in the discovery of North American tobacco and the subsequent successful introduction by John Rolfe in 1612 of the sweet oronoco variety from Venezuela, which greatly satisfied European tastes. By 1617, Rolfe had devised a system of curing which reduced spoilage on the trans-Atlantic crossing. Tobacco, as a cash crop, spread like a fever and even could be found growing in the streets of Jamestown. Thomas Dale, Virginia's royal governor, ordered all farmers to plant at least two acres of corn per person lest his constituents neglect growing enough staple crops to survive. The British Crown and Parliament, pleased with the potential of this new cash crop, required that tobacco be shipped to England before being distributed to the European continent. The Virginia settlers deemed this a promising monopoly with guaranteed markets. Among other things, it added to a planter's capacity for improvements in capital formation – houses, barns, orchards, and gardens. However, in reality, it marked the beginning of England's strategy for total control and manipulation of profits and revenue. As a result, Chesapeake society became increasingly dependent upon the success of one cash crop in order to import finished goods from across the Atlantic.[1]

Most early tobacco plantations in Virginia were located near navigable waterways so transporting the tobacco to a ship bound for London or Bristol remained relatively easy. From their initial settlements along the James River, Chesapeake planters began moving further inland in search of fertile land and settled on the banks of the York, the Rappahannock, and the Potomac. They constructed wharves to handle tobacco exports and to receive imports ordered from England.

There were drawbacks to the repeated planting of tobacco, however; it was hard on the land, depleting the soil and robbing it of valuable nutrients. For the growing population of planters with their single crop economy, the continuous cultivation of one field with tobacco for four years resulted in substantial soil exhaustion. In fact, it took some twenty years of lying fallow for the soil to regenerate. Only planters with extensive acreage and large numbers of slaves, consequently, could afford to cultivate new plots of land with tobacco while allowing exhausted fields to lie fallow or be replanted with English wheat. Small planters often exhausted their lands and moved on.

Unlike grain, tobacco cultivation was quite labor-intensive. Each plant was tended individually, from planting to weeding to harvesting. Therefore planters imported almost all goods – except food – in order to direct manpower towards the leaf's cultivation. For most Virginia planters, the early focus of their farming was the acquisition of cheap land and indentured servants, including convicts from England's Old Bailey and Newgate prisons. By the late 17th century, Virginia planters faced a decline in the availability of indentured servants and turned to slavery as a long-term investment in labor. The final decade of the century saw the introduction of more slaves into Virginia than in all previous years.[2]

Merchants in England usually sold Virginia tobacco on commission and the planters received extended credit based on a percentage of the gross sale. Under this arrangement, imported English merchandise, household furnishings, clothing, implements, and books, gradually added to an improved quality of plantation life. This was particularly true for the elite upper class of planters in Virginia who had strong familial, financial, and cultural ties with England and a desire to replicate as best they could the life of the landed gentry back home. In England, the age-old farming tradition had been replaced by a more commercial, market-based agriculture with capital investment by landlords and farmers. The Virginia planters viewed tobacco as their major investment. Unfortunately, the Virginia planter too often found his operating costs and the price of creature comforts greater than his profits from tobacco sales.

In spite of their problem with chronic debt, the planters expanded their estates. Progress was further measured by the power and position they enjoyed in their far-flung communities. These planters were proud of their houses, crops, gardens, animals, and libraries. Wealth, privilege, and status were essential ingredients to social and political advancement in Tidewater Virginia society.

Most Virginia planters were civic-minded, as well, and served as county officials, judges, militia leaders, members of the House of Burgesses, and church vestrymen. These posts contributed to their social status, and, in some instances, to their pocketbooks. Through personal contact, correspondence, newspapers, and books, these elite Virginians formed their perspectives on local, colonial, and world affairs.[3] It was in this environment, with a labor intensive cash crop economy, that young George Washington would grow up to become a prominent planter and influential member of the Virginia aristocracy.

In 1743, Augustine Washington died, leaving eleven-year-old George and four younger siblings at Ferry Farm, the Washingtons' home on the Rappahannock River across from the town of Fredericksburg, Virginia. Augustine had moved his family from Westmoreland County to the tract that would later be known as Mount Vernon, then relocated once again to Ferry Farm when George was about seven. It is not clear how much time the fatherless George spent divided between Ferry Farm and Mount Vernon, the new home of his elder half-brother, Lawrence. Yet through Lawrence Washington's marriage to Ann Fairfax, George formed a new family bond that would prove to be critically important to his early career development. Both Lawrence and Ann's father, Colonel William Fairfax, became young George's mentors in the areas of education, social manners, and public responsibility. George mastered arithmetic,

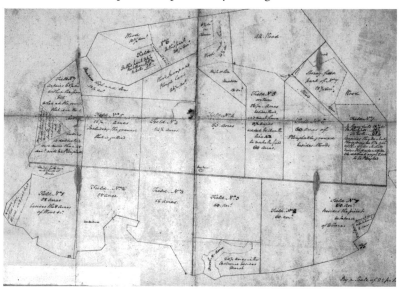

Washington consolidated his Ferry and French's Farms into Union Farm in the 1780s and used his surveying skills to lay out the fields.

geometry, trigonometry, and surveying. His school exercise books reflect his study of the practical aspects of daily life, including legal forms such as bills of exchange, tobacco receipts, land leases and patents, a servant's indenture, and a short will. Washington supplemented his early education by improving his writing and by additional readings in literature, geography, and history. With a basic knowledge of law and business, as well, young George Washington, under the tutelage of Lawrence Washington and William Fairfax, would progress along the responsible road of the landed Virginia gentry.

Throughout the colonies, land surveying was considered to be "a profitable and genteel pursuit" and one that George Washington took up with enthusiasm as a teenager, employed initially by Thomas, Lord Fairfax. Cousin of William Fairfax, Lord Fairfax was proprietor of over one million acres in Virginia's Northern Neck between the Potomac and Rappahannock Rivers. Fairfax employed surveyors to mark off these holdings. From 1748 to 1751, Washington honed his surveying skills in the Fairfax Land Office. During this period, Lord Fairfax took a special interest in Washington, encouraging him to use his library containing one of the finest collections of books in the colonies. Washington utilized Fairfax's library, secured a surveyor's commission, and went on to pursue a respectable and profitable, if short-lived, career in the profession. His more than 190 surveys reveal a special eye for changing terrain, potential travel routes, prospective town sites, and natural resources. For the remainder of his life, Washington would continue to draw upon his surveying skills to forward his own acquisition of new tracts. With the high value he placed on land, Washington pursued, as an individual and at times with partners, major purchases within and beyond the boundaries of Virginia.[4]

The land which garnered most of Washington's early attention was Mount Vernon, which came into his possession after Lawrence Washington's death. In 1754, he leased 2,300 acres, the dwelling house, and a gristmill from his half-brother's widow, and acquired the property outright at her death six years later. Keenly aware of the importance of obtaining additional contiguous land around Mount Vernon, Washington purchased strategically located parcels over the next twenty years. The expansion of the Mount Vernon property began in December 1757 when Washington purchased two parcels on the plantation's northern boundary from Sampson Darrell of Fairfax County. By 1787, Washington had consolidated the Mount Vernon estate into five farms: Mansion House Farm with 2,100 acres and an expansive view of the Potomac; River Farm with deep water access; Ferry and French's (later named Union) Farms with a potentially lucrative fishing enterprise; Dogue Run Farm with a gristmill; and Muddy Hole Farm. Support buildings on each farm included an overseer's house, slave cabins, separate corn and tobacco structures, fodder houses, livestock sheds and pens.[5]

Up at dawn, Washington rode daily to all his Mount Vernon farms communicating with overseers and observing the needs and progress of each day. To see and be seen on his farms remained an important part of Washington's management style. Under his detailed directions, a hierarchy of estate managers, overseers, indentured laborers, seasonal hires, and a growing slave labor force worked the farms, built the structures, raised the livestock, and carried out other daily tasks. The Mount Vernon estate grew in size, to nearly 8,000 acres, as did the number of slaves, from 36 in 1754 to 316 by 1799.[6]

The work day for slaves at the Mount Vernon estate extended from sunup to sundown with two hours for meals. The daily diet for field hands included one quart of cornmeal and five ounces of salted or pickled fish. During times of intensive work, slaves were provided fresh meat. At the end of a work day, on Sundays, and on holidays, slaves could tend their gardens, chickens and ducks, and also go hunting, trapping, and fishing as a means of supplementing their prescribed diet.

The overseer's responsibility was to manage and supervise the labor force at his farm. Washington stressed a strict relationship between the farm overseers and the slaves; he believed that being too familiar weakened one's authority. Washington counseled his farm manager, William Pearce, on the proper relationship in supervising the overseers of his four farms, stressing the balance of civility and proper distance. Washington provided this same advice to the farm overseers, each of whom was responsible for forty to fifty slaves and lived among them. Work, accountability, and efficiency were extremely important: "A penny saved is a penny got" and "many mickles make a muckle" were phrases to live by.[7] Washington encountered his share of challenges at Mount Vernon – the shortcomings of the slave labor system, incompetent and uninspired overseers, damaging weather and insects, shortfalls in crop production, broken-down farm tools and implements, failing yields, unaccountable losses of livestock – but, through it all, Washington maintained a sense of fairness and honesty in his dealings, and expected as much in return.

At first, Washington emulated the great planters whose rise in society was tied to the British tobacco trade. In 1757, he wrote to a London merchant stating that he expected to ship a large quantity of quality tobacco annually. In 1758 and 1759, he opened trade with the

Like most Virginia planters, George Washington attempted to make his fortune on tobacco. He would find, however, many shortcomings associated with the crop.

prestigious London business firm of Robert Cary and Company, and ordered fine china, silver, fashionable clothing, furniture, books, decorative porcelain, statuary, paintings, cloth, ceiling ornaments, and mahogany furniture for Mount Vernon. Over time, Washington learned firsthand the weaknesses of this method of trade. For instance, Washington and his fellow planters were the victims of hidden fees such as insurance against loss of cargo at sea, duties per hogshead of tobacco, freight charges, brokers' fees, and the commission retained by the commercial representative in London. After 1759, this "complicated system of duties" often ran as high as 80 per cent of the final sale.[8]

Ultimately, Washington's hopes to become rich from tobacco were never realized. Tobacco demanded the full attention of his field hands to pick off worms and pests, hoe weeds, and prune the plant to achieve a larger leaf; this left little time to pursue a more diversified husbandry. In addition, the clay soil at Mount Vernon could not produce tobacco of a quality competitive with that being cultivated and sold in southern Virginia. The shallow plowing and cultivation process necessary for tobacco also caused serious erosion problems. Faced with all the frustrations and disappointments that had plagued Virginia tobacco farmers for generations, Washington developed an interest in the "new husbandry" practices already under way in England and he began to seek out published information about the status of British agriculture.

From 1756 to 1760, Washington ordered several British agricultural books from England which had little or nothing to do with the cultivation of tobacco: Batty Langley's *New Principles of Gardening* (1728) contained a variety of garden designs including a kitchen garden for medicinal, cooking, and herbal uses; William Gibson's *A New Treatise on the Diseases of Horses* (1751) discussed the external parts of the horse including color, markings, and signs determining age; Jethro Tull's *The Horse-Hoeing Husbandry* (1751) provided descriptions of the four-coultered plow, the drill plow, and a comparison of old and new husbandry; Edward Lisle's *Observations in Husbandry* (1757) discussed manures, field implements, the sowing of grains and grasses, the nursery, and the care of farm animals; Thomas Hale's *A Compleat Body of Husbandry* (1758-1759) examined soils, uses and care of farm animals, and the cultivation of hops, hemp, and flax.

These and other works provided Washington with useful information about new crops, as well as improvements in livestock and crop rotation. By 1760, Washington was already implementing Tull's horse-hoeing techniques and cross plowing. He also conducted compost experiments with oats and barley, using river mud, horse dung, cow dung, marl, sheep dung, black mould, and clay.[9]

At this time, a young George III was on the British throne. Because the costly Seven Years' War (1756-1763) had produced a large national debt in England, a series of taxes on goods imported into the colonies was passed as a revenue-enhancing measure. Specifically, the Sugar Act (1764) and the Stamp Act (1765) imposed commercial taxes in the colonies similar to those in Great Britain. Because Parliament passed these acts without consulting the American colonies, seeds of discontent began to germinate. Between 1760 and 1764, in spite of having paid close attention to his tobacco fields, George Washington experienced a steady and disappointing decline in tobacco sales while, at the same time, he also faced high prices for what he deemed inferior British goods.[10] Washington found his dependence on a single cash export to the mother country unacceptable on economic and, increasingly, on political grounds. So, along with tobacco, Washington began to grow wheat as a cash crop. Between 1764 and 1770, Washington contracted with Alexandria merchants John Carlyle and Robert Adam to sell Mount Vernon wheat. His new crop venture translated into the following deliveries: 257 bushels in 1764; 1,112 bushels in 1765; 2,331 bushels in 1766; 1,293 bushels in 1767; 4,994 bushels in 1768; and 6,241 bushels in 1769.[11] Recorded diary entries for 1768 find him pursuing grain production throughout the year using cradlers, rakers, binders, and threshers, with carters hauling wheat in the summer.[12] Washington also began to pursue the domestic and foreign market options for the sale of other grains, hemp, and flax. In effect, Washington put into motion a reorganization plan at Mount Vernon which included abandoning the cultivation of tobacco along the Potomac and committing to a diversification of his cropping, which would, in turn, expand his market opportunities.

This enthusiasm extended to cloth production. Washington ordered spinning and weaving equipment so that he could eventually reduce reliance on costly imported clothing for his slaves. Between 1767 and 1768, Washington initiated a small cloth manufacturing

Washington, the Planter, original etching by Louis Conrad Rosenberg, 1932. Published by the American Art Foundation. Collection of the Mount Vernon Ladies' Association.

business at Mount Vernon, employing a white woman and five slave girls to spin and weave cotton, linen, and woolen cloth for both plantation use and sale. By the second year, this home industry had produced 815 yards of linen and 1,355 yards of woolen linsey and cotton, thereby reducing, if only minimally, the volume of imported clothing.[13]

By the time of the American Revolution, Washington owned an expanding and ever-changing farming enterprise. As Commander in Chief of the Continental Army he was absent from his fields for over eight years, a setback to his personal economy that he shared with many citizen-soldiers. Yet despite his intense preoccupation with the military and political challenges of the Revolution, Washington found time to write weekly letters of instruction to the manager of his plantation. Longing for home, yet focused on the vision of a new nation planting the seeds of peaceful opportunities, the General addressed his army at the end of the war, encouraging his troops to seek out the livelihood of their choice:

In such a Country, so happily circumstanced, the pursuits of Commerce and the cultivation of the soil will unfold to industry the certain road to competence. To those hardy Soldiers, who are actuated by the spirit of adventure the Fisheries will afford ample and profitable employment, and the extensive and fertile regions of the West will yield a most happy asylum to those, who, fond of domestic enjoyments are seeking for personal independence.[14]

Washington's own quest would lead him back home. In December 1783, a victorious Washington bid his officers farewell at Fraunces Tavern in New York, and resigned his military commission to Congress at Annapolis, Maryland. On Christmas Eve, Washington returned to his beloved Mount Vernon a war hero, eager to abandon public life and resume his agricultural pursuits with a renewed sense of inquiry and energy. Just a month after his homecoming, he wrote his comrade-in-arms, the Marquis de Lafayette: "I am not only retired from all public employments, but I am retiring within myself." He later wrote the Marquis' wife that he now looked forward to enjoying his private life, "with the implements of Husbandry, and Lambkins around me. . . ."[15]

At home, Washington found himself able to enjoy a cold and icy winter for the first time in almost a decade. Trapped by the snow, memories of Valley Forge fading, America's most famous private citizen reveled in the warmth provided by his family close at hand. With the breaking of spring and receipt of a letter from a nephew requesting a loan, the realities of making a living from the land hit hard. "I made no money from my Estate during the nine years I was absent from it," he wrote to his nephew, "and brought none home with me."[16]

Washington set out to reacquaint himself with the agricultural reforms occurring in England, generally known as the "new husbandry," especially the transition to a more market-oriented agriculture, as well as the latest agricultural literature emanating from this evolving agrarian revolution. He needed to explore the latest practices in animal and crop husbandry and examine updates in farm technology.

The determination to become a more successful farmer was matched by Washington's personal desire to learn, to experiment, and to implement the right action. During quiet times in the evening, Washington, the war hero, would sit down at his desk in the Mansion study as Washington, the farmer, to correspond with leading agriculturists in America and England concerning the latest developments and most useful books to purchase. Often, after pointing out the particular importance of a book or pamphlet, he would loan that title to his farm manager.[17] Corresponding with farmers from other regions and nations, as well as consulting agricultural works, expanded Washington's network beyond his informed Chesapeake neighbors.

As the small group of national and international agricultural writers grew so did the challenge of researching, sharing, and testing new scientific ideas and reporting the results. Washington carried on a lengthy and enlightened correspondence with Arthur Young (1741-1820), British agriculturist, author, and editor of the *Annals of Agriculture*. Young believed that each generation of farmers could benefit from the knowledge and advances of those who preceded them. Through Washington's reading and note taking from Young's *Annals* in such areas as grasses, grains, vegetables, cattle, manures, and plows, the Virginian became more convinced than ever of the superiority of the English system of new husbandry and concluded that the *Annals* could serve as a guide for improving farming throughout the United States.[18] Washington also came across Young's 1786 article "On the Conduct of Experiments in Agriculture" which explained how scientific trials might require months, even years, in an open field environment, weighing the variables of soil conditions and weather. As for Young's role in the process, he saw himself as an intermediary of "Immense and attentive discrimination" who could tour the farms of England and "turn . . . local practices into knowledge; assign the cause to the effect; and convert scattered observation into science, by deducing effective principles. . . ."[19] Washington admired the *Annals* because he thought that most agricultural treatises lacked the foundation of practical application. Washington expressed his reservations to Young:

> The System of Agriculture (if the epithet of system can be applied to it), which is in use in this part of the United States, is as unproductive to the practitioners as it is ruinous to the land-holders. Yet it is pertinaciously adhered to. To forsake it; to pursue a course of husbandry which is altogether different and new to the gazing multitude, ever averse to novelty in matters of this sort, and much attached to their old customs, requires resolution; and without a good practical guide, may be dangerous; because, of the many volumes which have been written on this subject, few of them are founded on experimental knowledge, are verbose, contradictory, and bewildering. Your Annals shall be this guide.[20]

It was with the same intense scrutiny that Washington studied the works of Jethro Tull, an English agriculturist; Henry Home, or Lord Kames, a Scotsman adept at farming and law; and Henry Duhamel du Monçeau, a most remarkable French economist and botanist.

Arthur Young, considering Washington to be as effective a farmer as he was a general, offered to obtain for him seeds and implements. In response, Washington asked Young to send him two English plows with extra shares and coulters, as well as superior varieties of seeds of cabbages, turnips, sainfoin, rye-grass, hop clover, winter vetches, wheat, field beans, spring barley, and oats. The fruitfulness of their trans-Atlantic friendship was reflected in Washington's diary entries for October 25, 1787 and for March 18, 1788, respectively: "At the

Crop rotation was one of the hallmarks of the new husbandry. This plan for Mount Vernon's Dogue Run Farm was outlined by Washington.

Mansion House setting Turnips raised from Seed sent me by Mr. Young to propagate Seed from" and "At Frenchs . . . 6 bushels of English Oats (sent me by Mr. Young) was sowed on abt. 2 Acres of grd."[21] With the exchange of new varieties, Washington was left with the task of determining which stocks would best thrive in the Virginia climate. In typical pragmatic fashion, he conducted tests. On March 31, 1787, for instance, Washington experimented with the sowing of oats:

> The East half of No. 2 with half a Bushel of Oats from George Town and the west half with a Bushel of Poland Oats – the east half of No. 4 with half a bushel of the Poland Oats and the West half with a bushel of the George Town Oats. The objects, and design of this experiment, was to ascert[ai]n 3 things – 1st. which of these two kinds of Oats were best . . . 2d. Whether 2 or 4 bushels to the Acre was best and 3d. the difference between ground dunged at the rate of 5 load, or 200 bushels to the Acre and ground undunged.[22]

At Mount Vernon, Washington raised over 60 crops and many – including clover, potatoes, corn, and wheat – involved experimentation and recorded observation.

Washington also wanted to learn more about the expanded systems of crop rotation then being applied in Britain and the United States. With this in mind, he took extensive notes from his copy of Henry Home's book, *The Gentleman Farmer,* first published in 1776. This treatise includes descriptions of agricultural implements, cattle and horses, soil preparation and fertilization, grass and plant cultures, reaping and storage of corn and hay crops, and crop rotation. Washington copied detailed sketches of two harrows, as well as tables of a six-year crop rotation plan for clay and free soil. The rotation entailed the practice of alternating fallow land (plowed and harrowed soil left unseeded for a growing season), wheat, peas, barley, soy, oats, and pasture. Washington noted from Home's work that he considered the proper use of crop rotation to be the most important aspect of good husbandry.[23]

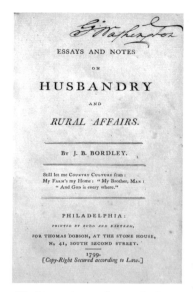

Washington's signed copy of John Beale Bordley's Essays and Notes on Husbandry.

In a neighboring state, Washington's good friend John Beale Bordley (1727-1804) was carrying out crop rotation experiments of his own at his 1,600-acre farm on Wye Island, on the eastern shore of Maryland. Like Washington, Bordley was an enthusiastic student of British experiments in agriculture; unlike Washington, he published the results of his research trials. In *A Summary View of Courses of Crops (1784),* Bordley compared the English Norfolk system of crop rotation with general practices followed in Maryland, and judged the latter inferior. In turn, Bordley offered his own eight-field system as an alternative solution to the problem of soil exhaustion. In his treatise, *Rotation of Crops,* Bordley discussed the old and new systems of crop rotation which were in practice in both England and America, including the planting of maize and clover seed and the sowing of wheat on clover. He also supplied plans for cattle stalls, barns, and ice houses. Washington studied these observations. He took notes from his first edition copy of Bordley's *Essays and Notes on Husbandry* concerning the use of various types of trees for shade in pasture land, as well as the use of clover and timothy in a particular rotation system. This work was considered one of the first published accounts of scientific agriculture in America.[24]

Washington encouraged Bordley and underscored the modeling role of the elite:

> Experiments must be made, and the practice (of such of them as are useful) must be introduced by Gentlemen who have leisure and ability to devise and wherewithal to hazard something. The common farmer will not depart from the old road 'till the new one is made so plain and easy that he is sure it cannot be mistaken.[25]

16

Through trial and error, Washington sketched out his own seven-year plan for Dogue Run Farm, from 1793-1799, including the use of buckwheat, corn, clover, grass, manure, and potatoes – illustrative of but one of his many efforts at diversified farming.

Considering the ongoing shifts in his crop base and cultivation techniques, Washington decided that it was necessary to implement a new division of labor, by sex, among his field hands. The men were made responsible for the concurrent operation of nine to twenty plows engaged in deep plowing and harrowing, while the women raked, gathered, bound, and carried the harvested grain. Women also grubbed the meadows and swamps, weeded the corn and vegetables, collected and spread the organic dung matter. A sampling of Washington's diary entries for April 16 and 25th, 1788, reflects a change in duties for female field hands:

> The Women having finished hilling as much grd. [ground] as would do for the Sweet Potatoes, I ordered them to remove the Farm Pen, & to heap the dung. . . . The drag harrow followd the Plows, and the Women (after they had spread the Dung there) followed the harrow, in order to knock the clods to pieces & remove the grass, to fit it for Oats – Clover & orchard grass.[26]

The divisions were not absolute for, on some occasions, females plowed and harrowed while elderly men and young boys helped them grub, pick peas, and make fences.

As an active proponent of the new husbandry, Washington also focused on the improvement of farm implements. As early as 1760, according to a diary entry, Washington indicated that he was trying to fashion a plow to fit the needs of his farm: "Spent the greatest part of the day in making a new plow of my own invention."[27] Years later, Washington successfully devised his own improved version of the barrel plow. Washington probably discovered the plans for this machine while reading his copy of Duhamel's *A Practical Treatise of Husbandry* (1762) or Young's *Annals of Agriculture.* By synthesizing his notes and his own experiences, Washington hoped that the barrel plow would prove useful not only at Mount Vernon but also on many farms throughout America.

Washington believed that the time-consuming process of seeding by hand and covering with a hoe, a drag, or harrow might be replaced with a farm machine capable of performing these tasks almost simultaneously. Washington's improved barrel plow consisted of a wooden barrel cylinder mounted over a wheeled plow. As a horse pulled the plow forward, the barrel turned. The barrel had holes cut or burned through in such a way that it allowed corn or other seeds to drop freely into tubes that ran down to the ground. On July 26, 1786, having placed a roller on the end of his drill plow and a brush harrow between the plow and the barrel, Washington's plow was successfully used at his Muddy Hole Farm. Colonel Theodorick Bland (1742-1790), a farmer in Prince George's County, Virginia and veteran of the Continental Army, made a visit to Mount Vernon and accompanied Washington to view some of the threshing and cutting activities at Muddy Hole. There is a good chance that Bland saw Washington's barrel plow in action. Through the remainder of the summer, Washington monitored the performance of his invention, making modifications. Washington must have been satisfied with the overall performance of the barrel plow for, a few months later, he wrote to Bland that it was "equal to your most sanguine expectations, for Indian Corn, wheat, barley, peas, or any other tolerably round grain. . . ."[28] In the interest of improved efficiency and increased profit, Washington remained committed to pursuing the latest farm technology. In his October 6, 1793 communication with farm manager William Pearce, Washington wrote:

> I am never sparing . . . in furnishing my Farms with any, and every kind of Tool and implement that is calculated to do good and neat work, . . . I shall begrudge no reasonable expence that will contribute to the improvement and neatness of my Farms. . . .[29]

Having the right farm implements and maintaining them in good working order presented a continuing challenge at Mount Vernon. When Washington hired a carpenter overseer, he insisted that he be responsible for making and mending tools and farm implements, as well as passing on his skills to the slave craftsmen:

> I would repeat my expectation that [James Donaldson] will take pains to teach those who work with him (especially Isaac and the boy Jem) in the *principles* of the several kinds of work they are employed in; particular in Carts, Wheels, Plows, Harrows, Wheel barrows, and such kinds of impliments as are used about a farm, or dwelling house. . . .[30]

As part of the renovation program at Mount Vernon, new threshing barns became a major priority. These structures would become visible symbols of Washington's attempts to tackle challenges with invention. Although Washington was in the process of diversifying his farming enterprises to reflect a more independent estate, his diary entries reflect his frustration over the uncontrollable elements of weather, disease and, at times, reluctant slave labor. Between 1787 and 1794, Washington had two extraordinary barns constructed at Mount Vernon; both were designed to increase the efficiency of his grain threshing operation. As wheat was his cash crop, it was imperative that, after the midsummer harvest, the grain be separated from the wheat stalks in a timely manner. Two customary methods of separating – or threshing – the wheat were available to Washington. Striking the wheat with a wooden instrument called a flail was commonly performed by laborers, free and slave, on large wooden floors centered in rectangular barns. The force of the hand-held flail knocked loose the grain. Another, ancient, method was known as treading. This involved laying the wheat outdoors in a large circle or oval and driving horses atop the wheat, their stamping hoofs performing the same task as the flails. Washington's friend John Beale Bordley, in a 1786 essay "Some Account of Treading Out Wheat," reported that the treading process using horses was generally practiced in the peninsular area of the Chesapeake, while the flail was the common tool used for threshing in the regions north of Maryland. Washington utilized both methods at Mount Vernon.[31]

At Washington's request, Arthur Young sent a plan "of the most complete and useful Farm yard," including a barn, for a farm of 500 acres. Washington chose to build in brick, rather than wood, and his slave craftsmen began construction at Mount Vernon's Union Farm.

The barn was a two-story rectangular structure with a large floor for threshing wheat with flails. In 1788, Jacques Jean Pierre Brissot de Warville, a French journalist and reformer, visited Mount Vernon and saw this new barn at Union Farm in advanced stages of construction. He described it as "a huge one . . . about one hundred feet long . . . to store all his [Washington's] grain, potatoes, turnips, etc. Around it he had also built stables for all his cattle, horses, and donkeys."[32] Because of Washington's extended absences from home during the presidency, his best plans often went awry. On a visit home, he was disappointed to see that his Union Farm barn was not being utilized at all in the way it was intended. On October 16, 1793, Washington shared his feelings on this regrettable situation with Henry Lee, pointing out that in spite of having "one of the most convenient Barns in this, or perhaps any other Country, where 30 hands may with great ease be employed in threshing . . . notwithstanding, when I came home . . . I found a treading yard not 30 feet from the Barn door, the Wheat again brought out of the Barn and horses treading it out in an open exposure liable to the vicissitudes of weather."[33] Undaunted by the resistance on his farms to potentially productive agricultural change, Washington had already developed his concept of a circular barn which would allow livestock to tread out wheat under cover.

John Beale Bordley, in his essay on treading wheat, provided drawings of circular treading floors located outdoors, usually surrounding a barn structure. As for treading under cover, Bordley vaguely alluded to two such instances. Whether or not Washington had seen a treading barn in his many travels is difficult to determine – there is no evidence that he did. However, his design of a two-story, 16-sided treading barn is certainly original to Washington and unique.

In October 1792, Washington wrote to his manager Anthony Whiting, providing him with detailed design drawings and a list of materials required for construction of the barn on Mount Vernon's Dogue Run Farm. The plans were forwarded to Thomas Green, the carpenter foreman. One of the objectives of this new design was to produce a cleaner and more marketable product, to remove the treading of wheat from a dirt barnyard and away from wind and rain. A second goal was to keep the grain secure. Because theft was a great concern to Washington, his plan called for barred windows on the lower level and he specifically ordered the installation of "a good lock . . . upon the lower door."[34]

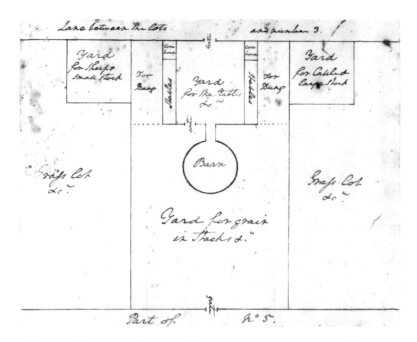

This plan of the 16-sided barn, stables, cornhouses, animal pens and barnyard was drawn by Washington to provide instructions to his manager concerning gates and fencing.

The "round" barn was built into an embankment, which allowed the horses to enter on the upper floor by way of an earthen ramp. The upper level floor was designed with 1½-inch spaces between the floorboards so as to allow the grain, separated from the straw in the treading process, to fall through to the lower level. On the lower level, the grain was shoveled or swept to the center, cleaned, then shipped in barrels or bags to Washington's gristmill, a short distance from Dogue Run Farm.

According to Washington's calculations, the foundation and first floor walls of the barn would require 30,820 bricks. Near the barn site a kiln was constructed and the slaves Muclus and Tom Davis headed the brick making and laying operations. The upper level was wood. The names of skilled slaves such as Gabriel, Isaac, and Simms appear on weekly carpenter reports which detail the preparation and installation of the pine and oak flooring, siding and framework.[35] Cautiously excited about the potential importance of his venture, Washington wrote his manager from Philadelphia:

> How does the treading floor in the new barn at Dogue-run answer? – Having tried it now in both Wheat and Oats, you must be enabled to decide, whether it is a more expeditious mode than to tread on the ground, or not. – That it is more clean and safe, if the lower door is always kept locked . . . can admit of no doubt.[36]

Washington's round barn, considered a milestone in American farm architecture, was so well-built that it would remain standing well into the 19th century. Existing records do not allow for a calculation of the barn's efficiency but, as part of Washington's continuing efforts to find creative solutions to age-old problems, it provided a fine example of a clean and secure approach to treading wheat, rye, and oats, thereby enhancing potential for profit.

Even while the Union Farm threshing barn and the Dogue Run treading barn were operating, Washington continued to consult with agriculturists at home and abroad on improved threshing techniques. William Booker, an agricultural inventor, visited Mount Vernon in July 1797 at Washington's request to build a manually-powered threshing machine of Booker's own design.[37] From the hand flail to the treading barn to Booker's portable machine, Washington continued to demonstrate his commitment to experimenting with new and more efficient farm technology.

The 16-sided barn was a complex structure of Washington's design, but the master of Mount Vernon also created a simple yet relatively rare building to support healthy crop yields. One of the key elements of progressive agriculture was the liberal use of fertilizers. In the 18th century fertilizers encompassed a wide variety of organic materials. At Mount Vernon, Washington used animal manure, fish heads and guts, marl, plaster of Paris and even mud scraped from the Potomac River. The importance of gathering and spreading fertilizer on Washington's fields is reflected in his letter describing the attributes of an exemplary farm manager: "When I speak of a knowing farmer, I mean . . . above all, Midas like, one who can convert everything he touches into manure, as the first transmutation towards Gold. . . ."[38] In order to compost organic material in anticipation of using it in his planting beds and fields, Washington sent instructions

Washington's 16-sided barn has been reconstructed at Mount Vernon using the same methods known to 18th-century craftsmen. During demonstrations, horses tread wheat in the barn.

to George Augustine Washington, his farm manager and nephew, to erect a "Repository for Dung," or "stercorary." This open-sided structure, about 31' x 12', had a floor covered with cobblestones. As he developed his plan for the repository, Washington may well have consulted his copy of Thomas Hale's *A Compleat Body of Husbandry* (1758-1759), which included an illustration entitled "The Plan of the Dung Pit." In its use, Washington may have turned for advice to a fellow agriculturist, John Spurrier. In his book, *The Practical Farmer* (1793), Spurrier recommended the types of waste and refuse to be integrated with animal manure in developing fertilizer. In June 1796, Washington directed that workmen "rake, and scrape up all the trash, of every sort and kind about the houses, and in the holes and corners, and throw it (all I mean that will make dung) into the Stercorary."[39]

The dung repository was located in a convenient location, adjacent to the Mansion House stables. Archaeological excavations undertaken in 1993 revealed that the floor and outline of the building bore a striking resemblance to a "Plan and Elevation of a Stercorary" submitted to the Philadelphia Society for Promoting Agriculture in 1808 by Judge Richard Peters (1744-1828), a friend who not only corresponded with Washington but also dedicated to the General his book, *Agricultural Enquiries on Plaister of Paris* (1797). Taken together, the historical and archaeological evidence documents the dung repository as an important innovation in Washington's conservation program.[40]

Washington's plan to increase the use of fertilizer on more than 3,000 acres of tilled land at Mount Vernon required a substantial commitment to a livestock program. Manure from cattle, horses, mules, and sheep was one of the farmer's most valuable assets. Of course, the animal population at Mount Vernon – extraordinary in its size and breadth for the period – also provided labor, food products, and raw materials, like wool and hides. While his greatest livestock interest remained his horses, sheep, and mules, Washington devoted considerable time to raising hogs, cattle, and poultry.

Horses

Washington had a special passion for horses. Thomas Jefferson considered him one of the finest horsemen of his time, and the French general Chastellux remembered that the Commander in Chief trained all of his own steeds. Prior to the American Revolution, Washington frequently hunted foxes on his Mount Vernon estate, often two and three days a week, following swiftly behind his own finely bred pack of hounds. And while he enjoyed attending horse races, and even owned an Arabian for this purpose, Washington valued horses primarily for their labor.

Washington established a breeding program for riding and work horses at the Mount Vernon estate at least as early as 1760. When his mares were not being bred or nursing their foals they could be found pulling plows or carts. On March 26, 1760, Washington completed work on his newly modified plow which he harnessed to his mares on the following day: "Sat my Plow to work and found She Answerd very well in the Field in the lower Pasture wch. I this day began Plowing with the large Bay Mare & Rankin."[41]

Hoping to improve on the breeding strain of his foundation stock Washington continually searched for promising mares. To this end, he bought 27 army mares used during the American Revolution. Shortly thereafter he acquired additional breeding stock in Lancaster, Pennsylvania. Quite possibly Washington was purchasing fine draft horses from German farmers in Lancaster County who, at this time, were breeding the first and most efficient American draft horse, the Conestoga, a regional breed used for pulling canvas-topped wagons over the tortuous mountain roads of Pennsylvania. This horse became a popular animal for farm use and commercial transportation in Pennsylvania.[42]

When Washington returned home at the end of the Revolution, compiling an inventory of all his livestock became a critical part of his future farm plans. In November 1785 he counted 130 horses in all, distinguishing between old or untrained horses and working animals, the latter numbering 57. At the Mansion House stable, he listed 21 horses, including riding horses Nelson and Blueskin, eight chariot horses, four wagon horses, four hack horses, two cart horses, and the Arabian stallion Magnolia.[43]

Washington took special pride in Magnolia. At five years old, the chestnut-colored, finely formed horse stood 16 hands high and carried popular bloodlines that could be traced back to the famous mare, Selima, by the Godolphin Arabian. Washington found this appealing since over thirty years earlier, on December 5, 1752, Colonel Benjamin Tasker, Jr. of Belair Farm in Prince George's County, Maryland, had journeyed to Virginia to race Selima against Tryall, owned by William

Washington and [George. William] Fairfax – Field Sports, H.B. Hall after Darley, n.d. Collection of the Mount Vernon Ladies' Association.

Byrd III of Westover. In one of the most celebrated inter-colonial horse races of the period, Selima won the race held at Gloucester, Virginia, taking the entire stakes of $10,000. Selima went on to achieve even greater fame as a broodmare.[44]

Injuries and illnesses tested Washington's skill as a stockman. When one of his horses was afflicted, Washington tried to find a remedy. His diary entries for February 1760 concern an injured wagon horse:

> Upon my return found one of my best Waggon Horses (namely Jolly) with his right foreleg Mashd to pieces which I suppose happend in the Storm last Night by Means of a Limb of a tree or something of that sort falling upon him. Did it up as well as I coud this Night. . . . Had the Horse slung upon Canvas and his leg fresh set – following Markhams [Gervase Markham, 1568-1637, author of several books on animal and crop husbandry] directions as near as I coud. . . . The Broken Legd. horse fell out of his Sling and by that means and struggling together hurt himself so much that I orderd him to be killd.[45]

It was an unfortunate ending but veterinary science at the time offered few options. Markham's directions indicating the use of a sling failed in this case. A more current work, *A New Treatise on the Diseases of Horses* (1751), by William Gibson, was also in Washington's library, but it did not provide information helpful for Jolly's serious injury. If the horse had recovered, the nature of his injury would probably have prevented him from ever regaining full use of the leg.

Sheep

Historically, early flocks of sheep in Virginia were established in the mid-1600s after a Spanish ship wrecked off the eastern shore of Virginia. Raised in a harsh and isolated environment, these hardy survivors carried Merino blood. According to George W. P. Custis, Washington's step-grandson, indigenous wild sheep also thrived in the protected environment of an island located off the eastern cape of

Virginia. Custis described a 2,000-4,000 acre island where sheep grazed year-round on herbage, grass, shrubs, and plants; they had ready access to available salt and took shelter in wooded areas. The name of the island and the origin of this stock was believed to lie with the Smith family who first settled the colony of Virginia. By 1650, the number of sheep in both Virginia and Maryland totaled only about 3,000.[46]

Washington's friend, John Beale Bordley of Wye Island, remembered that during the 1740s the rat-tail breed of sheep was raised in Maryland. Bordley described these sheep in his *Essays and Notes on Husbandry*, first published in 1799, as having small round tails and, at four and five years of age, producing "the best flavored mutton, dark, rich and juicy."[47]

By the middle of the 18th century, there were still comparatively few Virginia farmers raising sheep. George Washington, however, had a flock of over 100 at Mount Vernon as early as 1758. He valued them as a source of meat for consumption and for sale, fleece for spinning, and hides for tanning. By 1762, the flock had increased to 205. From his sheep inventories, it can be seen that Washington was a discerning breeder, choosing from each year's crop the few that he wished to keep as rams, the ewe lambs that he added to his breeding stock, the ram lambs that would be castrated to become wethers for meat and wool, and those to be immediately culled for meat.

Washington writes of breeding his flock of ewes in early October. Today, one good ram can breed about twenty-five to thirty ewes. Washington had a superior specimen. On October 6, 1766, according to his diary, he "Put my English Ram Lamb to 65 Ewes." With a five-month gestation period, lambing most likely occurred in March of the following year. Although Washington's diary for March of 1767 does not provide the results of the early spring lambing, it does include accounts of the weather which reveal unusually cold and wet periods during the first half of the month, including a number of days with frozen ground and either cold rain, snow, or hail. Facing such inclement weather conditions, Washington's new crop of lambs may have fared poorly.[48]

Despite Washington's long absence from Mount Vernon during the Revolutionary War, the 1785 livestock inventory indicates a small increase in the number of sheep to 283, but the retired General hoped to significantly expand his flock. At first, he looked to his neighbors to purchase stock. From William Fitzhugh, who owned estates in Northern Virginia and southern Maryland, Washington offered to buy up to 200 ewe lambs if they were available.[49] As would become custom, however, Washington made inquiries in Britain with the belief that in all matters of husbandry, English sources should be consulted. Washington discovered the achievements of Robert Bakewell, the renowned sheep breeder from Leicestershire.

Bakewell, by means of careful selection and inbreeding, had developed his own breed of sheep that would fatten for mutton at an early age with the least amount of bone and the least waste. His successes at his estate, Dishley Grange, were featured in Arthur Young's *The Farmers Tour Through the East of England* (1771). Washington may have read the comment by the correspondent in Northamptonshire, from Young's *Annals,* who referred to Bakewell as ". . . that very ingenious man [who] has the superiority of his breed to all others, beyond an idea of question or competition."[50] While Washington may have been excited by the prospects of this breed, he also knew that British statutes prohibited the export of Bakewells. Washington admitted that "less scrupulous" American farmers had succeeded in importing such rams. Although Washington did not engage in such activity, he was the recipient of lambs that had descended from Bakewells.[51]

For England, involved in the transition to a growing industrial population with expanded food needs, Bakewell's development of a faster growing, meatier sheep coincided with an increasing demand for mutton. In America, however, industrialization still remained in its infancy and the total population by 1790 had reached just under four million, with over 90 percent of all inhabitants employed in agriculture. Small-scale spinning and weaving, though, were a normal part of the home industry activities on the farm. At his Mount Vernon plantation, Washington was proud to claim that a sample of his wool had been sent to England where it was pronounced "to be equal in quality to the Kentish Wool."[52]

In October 1789, President Washington toured the New England states. He was impressed that the state of Connecticut, through the use of tax exemptions and bounties, had stimulated some successful spinning and clothmaking industry. This served to reinforce

Washington's desire for more successful production in Virginia. He wrote to Governor Beverly Randolph about the need for offering inducements to farmers, encouraging them to increase their quantity of sheep.[53]

As sheep raising expanded throughout the 1790s so did the problems of disease. One of the most common and serious diseases among sheep was foot-rot, a degenerative infection of the hoof. In his 1790 work entitled *The New England Farmer*, Samuel Deane (1733-1814), agriculturist and vice president of Bowdoin College, pointed out that "All wet moist lands are bad for sheep." Washington transmitted a summary of facts on American sheep in 1794 to the British Board of Agriculture and mentioned that foot-rot could be prevalent when sheep were confined in close quarters.[54] Washington's sheep operation always suffered the most when he was away from home and he wondered if the famous Bakewell sheep, placed under similarly unfavorable circumstances, would "soon degenerate for want of that care and attention which is necessary to preserve the breed in its purity." Despite detailed written instructions on the proper management of his sheep, Washington's unavoidable absences from Mount Vernon continued to coincide with a variety of problems associated with inattentiveness to his flock.[55] In April 1794, upon hearing that the lambing season had not gone well, Washington wrote to his farm manager:

> . . . at Shearing time, a selection of the best formed, and otherwise promising ram lambs [should] be set apart (in sufficient numbers) to breed from . . . let there be a thorough culling out, of all the old, and indifferent sheep from the flocks that they may be disposed of, and thereby save me the mortification of hearing every week of their death.[56]

His efforts to successfully maintain and expand his flock – at one point numbering at least 600 – were further plagued by the ravages of disease and wild dogs. Nevertheless, Washington believed that sheep, with all their problems, remained a worthwhile farming enterprise in the middle states of America.

Washington always maintained a good number of cows, bulls, oxen (adult castrated males), and calves at Mount Vernon. Having a reliable source to provide animal power for field work and to supplement the food supply remained vital to the long-term efficiency of the entire family operation. Washington's journals spanning the years 1761 to 1765 show him purchasing cattle and making decisions about the fattening of aged steers and oxen on oats. During this period, the size of the herd grew from 126 to 166 head of cattle. Because his oxen could wear the heavy equipment of the day and were more powerful than the largest draft horse, Washington used them in the field until the age of eight, then put them out to pasture for one year before slaughter. By November 1785, the number of draft oxen at Mount Vernon had reached 26. This total fluctuated since the goal was to maintain enough trained oxen to handle the difficult farm work, yet retire the animals to pasture and slaughter while the beef was still acceptable.

Washington made a practice of having all his cattle branded with the letters "GW" and his diary entry for November 1, 1765 revealed this routine being carried out on his farms:

> Sent 1 Bull 18 Cows & 5 Calves to Doeg Run in all–24 head branded on the left Buttock GW. Sent 3 Cows, & 20 Yearlings & Calves to the Mill, wch. with 4 there makes 27 head in all viz. 5 Cows & 22 Calves & Yearlgs. branded on the Right shoulder GW. Out of the Frederick Cattle made the Stock in the Neck up 100 head–these branded on the Right Buttock GW. Muddy hole Cattle in all [ ] head branded on the left shoulder GW.[57]

Washington probably owned the Devon breed of cattle. They provided not only draft work but also beef, veal, milk, and associated products such as butter, cream, and cheese. The Devon was originally brought to Massachusetts in 1623 from Devonshire, England. In New England, the oxen did the heavy work on the rolling rock-strewn fields. With limited available farmland to inherit or purchase, a number of New England's future sons ventured south with their stock to resettle on rich tracts in Pennsylvania. During the decades prior to the American Revolution, superior cattle stock from Pennsylvania was probably introduced into northern Virginia by the stream of settlers moving farther south in search of arable land.[58]

With Alexandria, Georgetown, and the developing capital city of Washington providing ready local markets, Washington considered the profit possibilities in establishing a dairy business at his estate. As early as 1760, there was a small dairy near the Mansion House kitchen, most likely dedicated to home consumption. In the spring of 1788, Washington ordered a dairy building constructed at his River Farm and later intended to build like structures at Union and Dogue Run Farms. Washington's papers indicate butter shortages at Mount Vernon and, in what would be his last instructions to his farm manager on December 10, 1799, he expressed his displeasure with the failure of his dairy operations. "It is hoped," he wrote James Anderson, "and will be expected, that more effectual measures will be pursued to make butter another year; for it is almost beyond belief, that from 101 Cows actually reported on a late enumeration of the Cattle, that I am obliged to *buy butter* for the use of my family."[59] Washington's writings do not reveal extensive attention to, investment in, or success at dairying as a business enterprise at Mount Vernon, but he certainly expected to fulfill the immediate needs of his plantation.

Hogs and Poultry

Washington raised hogs and pigs as a valuable source of food for all those living on the Mount Vernon estate. Hogs and pigs are both swine; they are distinguished only by their weight – hogs weigh over 120 pounds. In the summer, swine ran loose in the Mount Vernon woodlands, foraging for themselves. Unless there was a shortage of meat, the hogs were not taken for slaughter until they weighed nearly 140 pounds. Usually, they were gathered in autumn, penned up for fattening, then slaughtered for ham, salted pork, bacon, sausage, scrapple, chitterlings, and lard. Washington made detailed entries of the number of hogs slaughtered and their weights. In December 1785, for instance, 128 hogs were slaughtered at a total weight of over

17,000 pounds of pork. Thomas Bishop, an old servant of Washington's, and Thomas Green, carpenter foreman, each received 500 pounds of pork, while several farm overseers received slightly less than that, leaving over 15,000 pounds for the Washington family, the Mount Vernon slave force, "and the poor who are distressed for it."[60]

Although records indicated the number of hogs slaughtered, Washington was never certain exactly how many hogs he owned at any given time. As he noted in his November 1785 livestock inventory, "The Hogs at all the Plantations running in the Woods after the Mast [acorns], no Acct. could be taken of them." By 1792, Washington introduced the spirit of new husbandry into his hog raising practices, directing his farm manager to construct closed pens with plank floors, a roof, water, and good troughs for feeding and fattening. The fall of 1794 may have been a lean time in terms of the number of mature hogs available for slaughter at the Mount Vernon estate. Washington noted that as a general rule only the "full grown Hogs might be put up" but this particular year would require "the necessity of breaking in upon the young hogs" since he did not want to resort to purchasing pork.[61]

Washington also raised chickens, turkeys, ducks, geese, and a number of other birds for meat and eggs. For the many visitors approaching Mount Vernon, cackling and squawking filled the air. One guest, Jacques Jean Pierre Brissot de Warville from France, remembered his arrival there on horseback in 1788. After passing over two hills, he saw silhouetted on the horizon "a country house of an elegant and majestic simplicity." Soon he was close enough to hear the sounds of farm animals, especially the turkeys and geese.

The Mount Vernon collection included some interesting birds such as gifts in 1785 of "a Goose and Gander of the Chinese breed" from David Griffith (1742-1789), the first Episcopal Bishop of Virginia, and Chinese pheasants from the Royal Aviary of the Marquis de Lafayette.[62]

Mules

Washington was America's leading promoter of the breeding and use of mules, the offspring of a male jackass and a female horse (mare). The origin of Washington's title as "Father of the American

33

Mule" stems from a present bestowed by the King of Spain. In considering the possibilities of mule breeding, Washington penned a letter on July 18, 1784 to Robert Townsend Hooe of Alexandria. Hooe regularly sent merchant vessels to Spain and Washington inquired about the safety of transporting to America "a good Jack ass, to breed from." Upon learning of the American president's interest, King Charles III made arrangements for two Spanish jacks to be shipped to Washington as a gift. Hoping to introduce well-bred jackasses into America, Washington was elated by this news but, as the months passed, his sense of anticipation became tempered by increasing frustration. Finally, eleven months after the initial offer, Washington received a communication from the Lieutenant-Governor of Massachusetts, Thomas Cushing, that one of the jackasses had arrived in the port of Boston in the charge of a Spanish caretaker named Pedro Tellez.[63]

George Washington promoted the hardworking mule, a mainstay on American farms for 150 years.

Washington dispatched his farm manager, John Fairfax, to Boston. Return travel was to be overland and not to exceed the speed that the jacks could comfortably walk. The jackass – only one of the two survived the voyage – finally arrived at Mount Vernon on December 5, 1785. Washington wrote a letter to Florida Blanca, the Spanish Minister of State, expressing his appreciation to the King since such exportation was normally forbidden by Spanish law. Washington named the five-year-old animal "Royal Gift" in honor of the King. When measured on the portico at Mount Vernon, the jack was over 15 hands. During the first six months, Royal Gift refused to breed with the Virginia mares. Washington wondered if he was "too full of Royalty, to have anything to do with a plebean race. . . ." In time, Royal Gift's interest was aroused and he proved to be a valuable asset. Washington confided to Maryland farmer William Fitzhugh, Jr., that "I have my hopes that when he becomes a little better acquainted with republican enjoyments, he will amend his manners and fall into our custom of doing business."[64]

In 1786, Lafayette surprised Washington with a gift of a jack and two jennets (female jackasses) which arrived in the port of Baltimore from the Island of Malta. The Frenchman hoped the jackasses "will be less frigid than those of His Catholick Majesty." The new jack, named Knight of Malta, was smaller than Royal Gift. Washington described Royal Gift as "calculated to breed for heavy slow draught" and Knight of Malta for "Saddle or lighter carriages." From them both, Washington claimed, "I hope to secure a race of extraordinary goodness that will stock the Country."[65]

Washington experimented with mules on his farms, having them pull plows and double harrows in the fields and tracking their feed intake. He became convinced that the mules not only worked longer and harder than his horses but also required less feed. The dramatic switch from horses to mules at Mount Vernon is reflected in the livestock inventories. In 1785, Washington recorded 130 horses at Mount Vernon and no mules. In 1799, there existed 58 mules and only 25 horses.[66]

Word spread swiftly among the planter class in both Virginia and Maryland about Washington's mule breeding stock. In addition, Washington instructed manager John Fairfax to place advertisements about both jacks standing at Mount Vernon. Notices were posted in public places, such as courthouses, and published in the *Maryland Journal, Maryland Gazette, Baltimore Advertiser, Annapolis Maryland Gazette,* and the *Virginia Gazette.* One of these ads in the 1790s may have caught the attention of Frederick Skinner (1730-1811) of Calvert County, Maryland. Although tobacco and corn were his cash crops, Skinner's efforts at increased self-sufficiency included distilling, blacksmithing, and milling. His son, John Stuart Skinner (1788-1851), remembered his father sending his jennets over to Mount Vernon for breeding with Washington's jacks.[67]

Looking beyond the mid-Atlantic region, Washington also sent Royal Gift on a tour of the south for shows and arranged breedings. Although Royal Gift arrived back home tired, lame, and underweight, his tour was a success as reflected by a growing interest in mules as animal power. Washington's experimentation in mule breeding and his determination to promote its cost-effective value for the American farmer set in motion a major transition in the use of animals on the farm. By the 1880 census, the number of mules and donkeys in the United States had grown to almost two million.

Washington the Entrepreneur

When Washington switched from tobacco to mixed-grain cultivation, he broadened his base of income. Wheat, rye, and corn could be sold as raw commodities or could be processed into flour or meal. Washington attacked agriculture with a creativity that most American farmers – a very conservative lot – could not muster. To his career as a *planter* of one cash crop to a *farmer* of many, must be added the title *entrepreneur* of a major agricultural enterprise. His merchant gristmill, a whiskey distillery, and a substantial fisheries operation represent Washington's ability to scan the horizon of opportunity and to invest in enterprises that showed promise. At the same time, Washington was willing to risk his resources on new businesses in the hopes that they would provide a consistent income.

Milling

In 1754, when Washington first came to reside at Mount Vernon at the age of 22, the property included a gristmill dating to the 1730s when his father originally brought the family to the tract. This mill was most likely a two-story structure with a single set of grinding stones and a water powered wheel which was either an overshot wheel or a breast wheel. An overshot wheel was about 75 percent efficient and most suitable on sluggish waterways where a dam was built creating a high fall of water. A sluiceway carried the water to the top of the wheel where it entered the buckets, the weight of the water making the wheel turn. In the breast wheel, which was about 65 percent efficient and often depended upon a lock to regulate the flow of water it received, water was channeled into the buckets at a middle height and thus powered. There was also an undershot wheel which was only about 30 percent efficient. The type of wheel selected for use depended upon the site chosen for the mill and the millwright's preference.

In 1760, Washington temporarily assigned as his miller the slave Anthony who would be reassigned the following year to the carpenters and, by 1762, would become head slave carpenter. In his position as miller, Anthony advised Washington that the head of water provided an inadequate force when it fell on the water wheel. The old mill had so deteriorated that one day in April 1760 Washington timed its production: "I tried what time the Mill requird to grind a Bushel of Corn and to my Surprize found She was within 5 Minutes of an hour about."[68] Disappointed with the results and assessing the physical condition of the mill, Washington found himself faced with the need to make improvements. By October 1764, he had hired Robert Wright to make limited repairs. In the next few years, full-fledged wheat production was underway at Mount Vernon and Washington decided to replace his father's small plantation mill with a merchant mill capable of processing large quantities of high-grade flour suitable for sale in the colonies and for export to markets abroad.

In March 1770, Washington rode to the mill with his new millwright, John Ball, and selected a new site nearly one-third of a mile down Dogue Run from his father's mill where the tidal waters of the navigable part of Dogue Creek could flow up to the tailrace (that part of the race, flume, or channel that led away from the water wheel and returned the water to the stream). This would allow flat-bottomed boats to deliver grain to the mill or carry flour down to the mouth of the creek to a waiting brig or schooner bound for Alexandria, Norfolk, or more distant ports. When completed, the two and one-half story structure featured a breast wheel, 16 feet in diameter, housed inside the mill.

In February 1771, Washington purchased two pairs of millstones, hoisting gear for lifting barrels of grain and flour to the upper floors of the mill, and devices for sifting flour. The quality of the millstone determined the quality of the resulting flour. The stone's surface needed to be quite hard to keep its cutting edges, but not so rough that it would powder the wheat bran and result in flour that was less than white. Most country mills used local stone for the traditional coarse milling, but a miller striving to produce top quality flour would seek the best stones available which, at this time, were the buhr millstones from France. Consequently, Washington wrote to Robert Cary & Co. in London asking the firm to locate "a pair of French Burr Millstones" so his new mill could produce a superfine flour.[69] Specially made, quite expensive, and difficult to install, the buhr millstone was uniquely crafted from freshwater quartz, which held an edge significantly longer than other stone types. In this same year,

Washington also completed a new millrace – the canal for water to flow to the mill wheel – combining the flow from the main stream of Dogue Run and its tributary, Piney Branch Run. He observed that the race "seemed to offer Water enough for both [sets of millstones]. One of which [is] constantly employed in Grinding up my own wheat."[70] Records show that Washington's mill produced superfine flour; shorts, a by-product of wheat milling that consists of bran, germ, and coarse meal; middlings, any of various products of commodities of intermediate quality or grade; and bran, the skin or husk of grains of wheat, rye, and oats separated from flour by sifting.

The construction of the new mill and improvements in milling operations at Mount Vernon were critical for reducing Washington's own dependency on Great Britain. Income sources were varied. Not only could Washington sell flour ground from Mount Vernon wheat, but also when the market price rose he could purchase grain from neighboring farmers, add value by processing it into flour, and sell it in casks stamped with his initials. He also milled his neighbors' wheat, accepting one-eighth of their grain in return as was the custom.

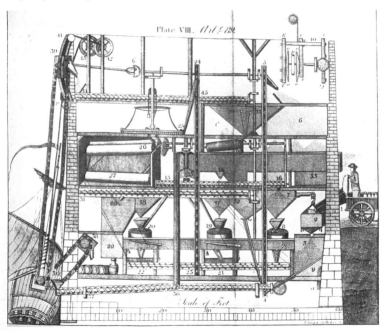

Illustration from Oliver Evans, The Young Mill-Wright and Miller's Guide, *depicting the author's method for efficiently circulating grain throughout a gristmill.*

In 1783, a fundamental change in milling technology occurred when Oliver Evans (1755-1819), an inventor from Newport, Delaware, designed machinery that dramatically reduced the manual labor required at a typical mill. Mechanical conveyors – driven by the water wheel – moved wheat, meal, and flour throughout the building. The product was carried in vertical bucket elevators, eliminating the heavy lifting of grain and flour packed in casks and barrels. An operation that required five men would now require two. An additional feature, a mechanical rake called a "hopper boy," spread the meal on the top floor to cool. During the years 1786 and 1787, both Maryland and Pennsylvania granted Evans exclusive rights to sell his new innovation.[71]

Evans's mill epitomized the efficiency Washington sought in all his endeavors. While some millers did not embrace it – as it threatened to put them out of work – Washington was among the first in line to pay Evans his license fee. In fact, Washington had the system installed in his mill four years before the publication of Evans's book, *The Young Mill-Wright and Miller's Guide* (1795). Evans provided detailed drawings of the system in his book. Washington contacted Evans and arranged for Evans's brothers to travel to Mount Vernon to oversee the installation in autumn 1791. Washington's ledgers indicate that he paid them for 20 days of work.[72]

Throughout these many years of continued efforts to improve milling operations, one question remained paramount in Washington's mind when he wrote his farm manager: "What quantity of flour is ground?" Alert to market conditions, however, Washington knew the question was not always that simple. In 1794, he instructed his manager William Pearce to thresh the wheat immediately and then sell it. There were two possible sale products: unprocessed grain or the grain ground as flour. To determine which would prove more economically advantageous, Washington asked Pearce to conduct an experiment and send one hundred bushels of medium quality wheat – "neither your *best* nor *worst* wheat" – to the mill to be processed. Washington requested that the resulting flour and bran be taken to the market at Alexandria and a price comparison made against a like amount of the raw commodity. He was inclined to believe that the unground wheat would bring a higher sale price than the flour. After giving the matter additional thought, Washington further advised

Pearce to discover whether the market at Alexandria sold wheat "by measure or by the weight" for, as he stated, "if 60lb. is called a bushel, and the wheat weighs only 55lb. the difference will be very great when a 100 bush[e]ls by measure is reduced to the bushels it will yield by weight at 60lb." Soon thereafter Pearce sent Washington the results of the experiment – that the flour had proved more profitable than the unprocessed grain – and in Washington's next communication, he asked that "the particulars" be forwarded to him. As farmer as well as entrepreneur, Washington regularly faced situations which required him to weigh production and profits.[73]

In the final analysis, receiving a fair price for his flour in the domestic and foreign markets was the measure of the mill's success. During the 1770s, the colonies had exported 751,240 bushels of wheat and 458,868 barrels of flour. There was demand for flour in England as well as in the local markets of Fredericksburg and Alexandria. In May 1771, Washington sold 13,500 pounds of flour to Robert Adam & Co. of Alexandria, three-quarters of which was fine quality. In June, this same merchant bought an additional 128,000 pounds of the same fine quality flour from Mount Vernon. Two merchants from Norfolk – a baker, Philip Carberry, and a West Indian trader, William Chisholm – purchased 1,432 pounds of ship stuff, the lowest quality flour containing much bran, and 36,997 pounds of fine flour, respectively. In July, 200 barrels of Washington's flour sailed aboard a brig to Jamaica while a ship left for Lisbon carrying 2,269 barrels. The following year, arrangements were made to ship some of Washington's flour to the West Indies on board the brig *Fairfax*.[74]

In the last two decades of the 18th century, Europe was in the throes of famine and war. Major harvest failures occurred in 1783, 1788, and 1795, weakening the Continent's ability to feed its people. The French Revolution had begun in 1789 and by 1793 Europe was locked in a deadly struggle between revolutionary France and their foes from Great Britain and Prussia. With the resumption of peace in America and the subsequent catastrophes of war and social revolutions in Europe, entrepreneurs in America saw a short-term opportunity for increased trade and profit without the burden of foreign competition. It was hoped that wheat would be one of the profitable commodities. In fact, American wheat and flour exports did increase during a brief window of opportunity between the years 1791 and 1793. As president, Washington chose a neutral path for the United States. As businessman, he hoped to take advantage of the grain and flour shortages in war-ravaged Europe. Between 1794 and 1799, these market demands were somewhat tempered as many American ships on the high seas were seized by the French and British navies.

Throughout this tumultuous period, Washington somehow found time to brief his farm manager regarding the impact of the European war on the price of flour and, in particular, its meaning for his own milling operations. In his April 6, 1794 communication to William Pearce, Washington expressed his concerns:

> I had no doubt but that the late capture of our Vessels by the British Cruisers, followed by the Embargo which has been laid on the Shipping in our Ports, w[oul]d naturally occasion a temporary fall in the article of provisions; – yet, as there are the same mouths to feed as before; – as the demand, consequently, will be as great; – and as the Crops in other parts of the world will not be increased by these means, I have no doubt at all, but that, as soon as the present impediments are removed the prices of flour will rise to what it has been. . . .[75]

It is clear that to optimize his chances for making the gristmill a profitable undertaking, Washington paid close attention to local, national, and international markets. In addition, he was willing to invest in technological expansion, as evidenced by Oliver Evans's machinery. Washington even attempted to establish subsidiary grain-based enterprises, including a whiskey distillery.

Washington's Distillery

Between 1700 and 1776, a large wave of Scotch-Irish immigrants sailed to America from Ulster and northern Ireland. With them they brought the knowledge of distilling whiskey from rye and corn. The first mention of a still at Mount Vernon appears in the invoice records of goods ordered by Washington and shipped from London between

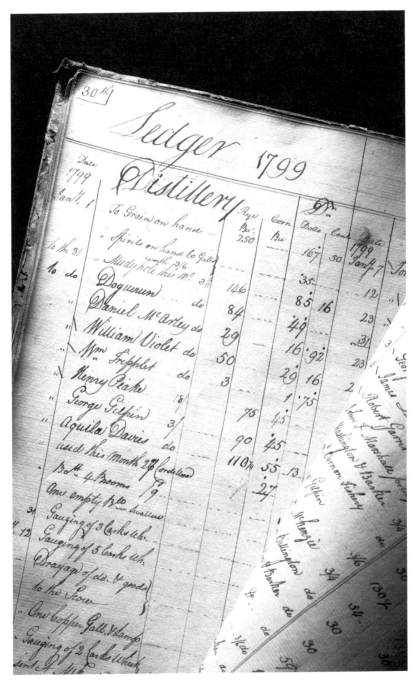

In Washington's farm ledger, accounts are kept of local customers – merchants, neighboring farmers, family and overseers – in view of tracking the economic success of the whiskey distillery at Mount Vernon.

1754 and 1766. Much later, in correspondence between Washington and farm manager William Pearce in August 1794, Pearce apparently asked Washington if the still could be used and Washington gave his assent although nothing beyond the original inquiry seems to have transpired. Pearce left Washington's employ at the end of 1796.[76]

James Anderson, who replaced Pearce, was an enterprising Scotsman who quickly assessed Washington's agricultural operation, as well as the ready availability of running water, and proposed that Washington build a distillery for corn and rye whiskey. Anderson enticed his employer with the promise of revenues derived from sales of the spirits and pointed out that the residuals from the distillery operation, such as corn cobs and mash, would provide excellent food for fattening hogs, which could be penned at the distillery site. He concluded by citing his expertise in the making of whiskey.

Washington admitted that he was completely unfamiliar with the distilling business. He thought the hog operation a "very desirable branch of the business" and after some initial trepidation gave Anderson his approval. Washington preferred to have the distillery built near his Mansion or Anderson's house in order, among other things, to discourage unwelcome visitors or robbers. When Anderson explained, however, the need for a water source for the distilling process, Washington gave his permission for a site on Dogue Creek near the gristmill.[77]

After consulting Alexandria businessman John Fitzgerald on his experience with distilling molasses, Washington proceeded with great exuberance. He ordered built a stone still house, 75' x 30', with a strong cellar to lock up the spirits, and a small malthouse. He furnished them with five copper stills, boilers, and tubs or vats. Wooden troughs were constructed to channel water from the creek to cool the vapor of the heated mash.

Barely a year into the operation of the distillery, Anderson hinted that he might leave Washington's employ. This disturbed Washington greatly, especially, he wrote Anderson, "after having induced me to encounter a very serious expence in erecting a Distillery of which I had no knowledge, nor the smallest intention to do, depending on your experience and judgment to carry it on."[78]

Anderson changed his mind and his son, John, was placed in charge assisted by six slaves. In March 1798, Washington wrote to

Samuel Davidson, a Georgetown merchant and land speculator, inquiring whether he knew of "some person of sobriety and good character, in whose integrity reliance can be placed" who could be hired as assistant to young John Anderson and trained, in time, to assume the responsibility of manager.[79]

Arrangements had to be made to acquire some of the raw materials needed to make whiskey. Washington had limited the growth of corn at Mount Vernon. He wrote his nephew, William Augustine Washington, that "My lands are not congenial with this Crop, and are much injured by the growth of it . . . Nothing but the indispensable use of the food for my negros (and indeed for Hogs) has restrained me from discontinuing the growth of it altogther. . . ." Washington hoped to arrange the purchase from his nephew of 500 barrels of corn annually, some of which he could direct toward corn whiskey production.[80] Ever mindful of market prices and how they might be affected by undulating national and international demands, Washington preferred to sell his grain products for cash instead of demanding a higher price in exchange for credit. He suggested to his nephew that he do the same. This topic also arose in Washington's correspondence to James Anderson, who had not succeeded in a recent bout with the corn market:

> You have an example before you of loss in the purchase of corn, & fall in the price of Whisky. Corn that I give 17, and 18/ a barrel for about Xmas, might afterwards have been purchased for much less. - I attach no blame to you on this account, and only mention it to show that one may be too fast, as well as too slow. . . . As to the profits of the Distillery, it is very probable I shall say nothing more about it until the close of the year, when – according to the proverb – the proof of the pudding will be in the eating.[81]

Acting on Anderson's early suggestion, Washington had hog pens built at the distillery. While the whiskey agreed with the palates of men, the corn cobs and mash agreed with swine. A Polish visitor to Mount Vernon in June 1798, Julian Ursyn Niemcewicz, commented

45

that the distillery operation offers "the most delicate and the most succulent feed for pigs . . . [They] are so excessively bulky that they can hardly drag their big bellies on the ground."[82]

As to the success of Washington's distillery venture, Anderson predicted that he would make at least 80 gallons per week. Apparently, the production and sales exceeded Anderson's calculations. In 1799, records reveal that almost 11,000 gallons of whiskey were produced at the distillery. In one of Anderson's initial letters to Washington, he suggested that it might be wise to deposit some of the whiskey in the cellar in anticipation of the labor-intensive fishing season for, "when the fishing Season comes there will be more demand and probably it will sell higher." Given the long established tradition in the colonies of consuming alcoholic beverages, the distillery could expect ready, and mostly regional, customers.[83]

The Mount Vernon Fisheries

One of the earliest references in Washington's writings of his attempts to fish the mighty Potomac River is a diary entry in January 1760: "Hauled the Sein and got some fish, but was near being disappointd of my Boat by means of an Oyste[r] Man who had lain at my Landing and plagu[e]d me a good deal by his disorderly behaviour." Several days later, as the Mount Vernon slave force continued to drag the nets, or seines, the "Oyster Man" continued his unspecified misconduct until he finally, begrudgingly, obeyed the young Colonel Washington's orders to leave.[84] Territoriality is nothing new to fishermen and it took Washington several years to establish his fisheries operation on the shoreline that stretched in front of his home.

Throughout the first half of the 18th century, the Potomac River had been a unifying force and a highway for travel and trade for citizens on both sides of the river, especially with the assistance of small water travel businesses and ferries linking Maryland and Virginia. Although the settlers of Virginia and Maryland utilized the Potomac to supplement their families' food supply, fisheries as profit-making enterprises were slow to develop. By the middle of the 18th century, however, the opportunities provided by the Chesapeake Bay and the Potomac River began to receive serious attention.

Washington described the Potomac as being "well supplied with various kinds of fish at all Seasons of the year; and in the Spring with the greatest profusion of Shad, Herring, Bass, Carp, Perch, Sturgeon &ca. Several valuable fisheries appertain to the estate; the whole shore in short is one entire fishery."[85] The waterway offered an opportunity to develop a fishery enterprise at the Mount Vernon estate which would provide greater self-sufficiency as well as an income – self-sufficiency because the fish would provide a source of meat for the slaves and income because there would be profits derived from the sale of salted fish, locally and abroad. Eventually, there would be at least three excellent fishery sites along the Mount Vernon shore with the most important at "Posey's Landing," where a ferry also ran across to Marshall Hall, Maryland. With the rental and eventual purchase of Captain John Posey's plantation, as well as another fishery further up the Potomac, Washington soon owned waterfront approaching ten miles in length. Every spring, herring and shad swam up the rivers of Tidewater Virginia and Maryland in order to spawn near the Great Falls. At opportune moments during those few short weeks when the schools were running, Washington's slaves stretched nets – some hundreds of feet in length and up to 12 feet in depth – across the water. This was an annual event for which all hands at Mount Vernon – slaves, indentured servants, overseers – dropped their work to help in the intensive fish harvest. The first of the catch was salted and packed into barrels to feed the slaves at Mount Vernon for the remainder of the year. The surplus was sold. Washington also allowed the poor in the neighborhood to fish from his shoreline for free if they first obtained permission from an overseer.

Washington soon realized that the success of his fishery operations depended upon reliable equipment. As early as March 15, 1760, an invoice from Robert Cary and Company indicates that Washington had ordered two new fish seines made of the best quality twine and measuring 35 fathoms in length and 20 feet in depth. Given the rigorous use and heavy wear, repairs and maintenance were both a priority and a continuing necessity. On July 2, 1769, Washington made arrangements with Captain Burch of the *Burmudian* to buy 562 barrels of salt, a cotton line, and 40 yards of nautical rope. Washington's diary entries show him visiting his fisheries often, no doubt to watch his boatmen draw the seines ashore by ropes around windlasses, devices

The Potomac River supplied Mount Vernon with shad, herring, carp, sturgeon, and other fish. Salted herring was a staple for the slave force and a marketable commodity.

for raising or hauling. In order to maximize his profits, Washington also paid close attention to his operating expenses, including such items as barrels and boats.[86]

The routine challenges of the fishery business began in January with the examination of all equipment, repairs, and the placement of orders for new materials and tools. Any of these tasks, if left unattended, could lead to problems. Unpredictable incidents, too, shadowed the fishing business such as cold and windy Aprils and an occasional light harvest. In 1786, Washington faced a disastrous spring fishing season. No doubt deep disappointment lay hidden beneath the terse comment preserved in his diary entry for May 13: "Ordered my People to quit hauling, and bring home my Seins."[87]

Beginning as early as 1760, though, Washington's successful management of his fisheries' business had stimulated additional income. According to successive diary entries from 1760 to 1770, the process of hauling seines in April and May remained relatively unchanged but the bounty increased tremendously. In 1772, in fact, one and a half million herring were hauled ashore to be salted and barreled for export.

At the close of the 1760s, trade in salted fish from the Northern Neck of Virginia to the West Indies was ready for expansion. Between 1769 and 1770, Washington arranged with Captain Lawrence Sanford to ship herring to the West Indies and Jamaica on board the brig *Swift*. In 1771, another shipment of Washington's herring reached Jamaica. For Washington, receiving payment for his fish often proved far more difficult than their preparation, packing, and shipping. In the summer of 1772, Washington sent a cargo of herring to the West Indies in the care of Daniel Jenifer Adams on board the *Fairfax* owned by Alexandria merchant John Carlyle. Adams sold the herring, bought the brigantine from Carlyle, and sailed about trading along the Atlantic coast for over a year without reimbursing Washington. When finally successful in bringing Adams to court, Washington was unable to obtain monetary compensation, although he *did* obtain the brigantine. He promptly renamed the ship *Farmer*, loaded her with another shipment of herring, and sent her back to the West Indies.[88]

Through his daily attention to the fisheries when at home and through his farm manager when he was absent, Washington was able to realize significant long-term success. During the 1790s, the fisheries even fared better than milling and other enterprises. Of all Washington's commercial ventures, his fisheries remained the most consistently profitable.

From the time he was 16 years old, when he noted the "sugar trees" on his surveying trips west of the Blue Ridge Mountains, George Washington was a meticulous observer of the landscape. His journeys to and beyond the western fringes of America's territories and his tours of every state in the Union as president provided Washington with a national vision that few of his contemporaries could comprehend. Wherever he traveled, Washington recorded not only the richness of America's agricultural potential but also marginal areas and the undesirable results of the wasteful practices of many farmers. Aware of his international reputation and willing to take advantage of it, Washington seized opportunities to communicate with his fellow farmers and promote the new husbandry by sharing the results of experiments and ideas for improving agricultural practices. Washington was not alone in his desire to improve agriculture in America. There were leading agriculturists abroad as well as at home who wanted America – the nation of democratic farmers – to succeed.

From overseas Washington's national outlook was supported by Sir John Sinclair, a Scottish landowner and patron for the British Board of Agriculture. Agricultural organizations were the vehicles of the day for discussing the status of farming and advocating improvements. Sinclair, in correspondence with America's first president, pointed out the need for establishing both state and local agricultural societies throughout the United States, as well as a national board of agriculture. Similar societies in England had already proven themselves to be instrumental in promoting new knowledge. Within the United States, the heavily cultivated and populated land along the eastern seaboard had already accentuated the need for such societies. The American Philosophical Society, which was organized in 1743, provided a model to emulate. As early as 1766, the New York Society gave substantial attention to the improvement of agriculture. Nine years later, in 1775, a number of farmers in Pennsylvania had reportedly expressed interest in establishing a similar agricultural society.[89]

Another ten years passed before the first organization to be concerned exclusively with the promotion of agricultural reform in

America was finally established in Philadelphia – the Philadelphia Society for Promoting Agriculture. The preliminary work on the formation of this organization was begun during the winter of 1784-1785 by a group of prominent men among whom were such notables as John Beale Bordley and John Cadwalader (1742-1786). During these winter months, Bordley, the experimental farmer from Talbot County, Maryland, spent a great deal of time in Philadelphia while John Cadwalader, a Philadelphia businessman, resided part-time at Shrewsbury, his estate in Kent County, Maryland. Bordley and Cadwalader became friends and visited one another in town and country, creating an organizational framework.

The Society itself was partly based on European models. Its early members were concerned with the state of agriculture in America, more specifically with what was believed to be "our great inferiority" and the need for "more skillful and fortunate management." Meetings were held at Patrick Byrne's Tavern, "Sign of the Clock," until June 1785 when they were moved to Carpenters' Hall. The Society embarked immediately upon a plan to acquire outstanding works on agriculture for its library. On May 14, 1785, founder John Beale Bordley presented to the Society 60 copies of his work *Summary Views on the Course of Crops in Husbandry of England and Maryland* (1784). Two years later, on July 3, 1787, George Washington attended a meeting at Carpenters' Hall. Acting on behalf of Arthur Young, he deposited with them six volumes of Young's *Annals of Agriculture*.[90]

The Philadelphia Society for Promoting Agriculture not only expanded its membership but also forwarded the cause of the new husbandry by publishing and distributing important essays on various aspects of agriculture and communicating with the common farmer. By 1789, the Society's membership began to assume a national dimension for, in addition to the some 23 Marylanders, it included individuals from Delaware, Kentucky, Massachusetts, New Hampshire, New York, Rhode Island, South Carolina, and Virginia.[91] The Society selected various communications pertinent to the advancement of agriculture for publication in monograph and article form to be included in almanacs, newspapers, and other periodicals. For example, there was the pamphlet entitled *Agricultural Enquiries on Plaister of Paris* (1797) by Judge Richard Peters, a practical farmer and the Society's first president. Peters had collaborated with Bordley and

President Washington as captured by artist Charles Willson Peale, circa 1795. Collection of the Mount Vernon Ladies' Association.

other members of the Society in establishing a number of model farms in Pennsylvania for the testing of grains, plants, shrubs, and trees.

In the preface to his pamphlet, Peters stressed the need to establish a state society of agriculture which would encourage communication, experimentation, and recognition for valuable ideas and deeds. He expressed dismay, however, at the "ineffectual" attempts by former legislatures, consisting mostly of farmers, to encourage research in agriculture. In the hope of stimulating some improvements, Peters contrasted these conditions with the "incalculable" advantages gained in England, as a result of its Board of Agriculture, and in France, where support for the advancement of agriculture was national policy. Peters corresponded with Washington and ultimately dedicated this small volume to him. Washington, appreciating this gesture, asked Peters for several additional copies.[92]

The Philadelphia Society found the press a particularly important medium for the dispersal of new husbandry ideas. In its June 8, 1787 issue, *The Pennsylvania Mercury and Universal Advertiser* carried the reprint of a letter to the Society from Colonel George Morgan, farmer and owner of "Prospect," a 300-acre farm which is now part of the Princeton University campus. Morgan proposed the establishment of a committee to conduct on-site inspections of a number of fields infected by the Hessian Fly and to develop preventive measures. The Hessian Fly, a destructive insect first appearing in Long Island, was reportedly brought into this country in the straw bedding used by Hessian soldiers.[93] In a limited way, the Philadelphia Society did become a vehicle for communication of progressive ideas although the Society had little or no influence over many small proprietors or yeomen farmers who continued to follow traditional methods.

Washington, an honorary member of the Society, noted that it promised "extensive usefulness if it is prosecuted with spirit."[94] He remained hopeful that agricultural societies would develop throughout America and share useful information, words of encouragement, and personal advice. On March 25, 1786, Washington wrote to William Drayton (1732-1790), who had recently informed Washington of his honorary membership in the South Carolina Society for the Promotion and Improvement of Agriculture. Washington's words of wisdom came with a warning:

> Nothing in my opinion would contribute more to the welfare of these States, than the proper management of our Lands; and nothing, in this State [Virginia] particularly, seems to be less understood. The present mode of cropping practised among us, is destructive to landed property; and must, if persisted in much longer, ultimately ruin the holders of it.[95]

Washington could often be found in quiet moments with pen in hand writing foreign dignitaries about the enormous future potential of America. To Sir Edward Newenham (1732-1814), an Irish politician representing Dublin in the Parliament, Washington described America's abundance: "We have an almost unbounded territory whose natural advantages for agriculture and Commerce equal those of any on the globe." To his good friend Lafayette, who had always been fascinated with America, Washington was just as effusive. "I hope, some day or another," he wrote, "we shall become a storehouse and granary for the world."[96]

These sentiments reflected Washington's finest hopes for the future of American agriculture but the fulfillment would require vigilance. From a lifetime of traveling throughout America, Washington knew firsthand how numerous farmers were perpetuating ruinous cultivation practices with no real effort at conservation and it appeared that time for positive change was running out. In a December 1791 letter to Arthur Young, he expressed his concerns with a sense of urgency:

... the aim of the farmers in this country (if they can be called farmers) is, not to make the most they can from the land, which is, or has been cheap, but the most of the labour, which is dear; the consequence of which has been, much ground has been *scratched* over and none cultivated or improved as it ought to have been: Whereas a farmer in England, where land is dear, and labour cheap, finds it his interest to improve and cultivate highly, that he may reap large crops from a small quantity of ground. That the last is the true, and the first an erroneous policy, I will readily grant; but it requires time to conquer bad habits, and hardly anything short of necessity is able to accomplish it. That necessity is approaching by pretty rapid strides.[97]

At the national level, President Washington's efforts to evoke support for the promotion of the new husbandry had little immediate effect for, at the time, there were far greater national and international challenges which demanded the attention of Congress. In 1794, Washington admitted this in a letter to Sir John Sinclair. "It will be sometime, I fear before an Agricultural Society with Congressional aid will be established in the Country; we must walk as other countries have done before we can run."[98]

Yet Washington kept on course. In his last annual address to Congress, he recommended that public funds be appropriated to assist in the development of a National Board of Agriculture for the purpose of collecting and disseminating agricultural information. He would ask Sinclair to advise and assist future members of the proposed Board in its establishment and implementation.[99]

Washington's proposed National Board of Agriculture did not receive funding in his lifetime but the idea endured through the years due in part to the continued efforts of agricultural societies. Throughout the first half of the 19th century, interest in the improvement of agriculture in America continued to grow at both the state and local levels where an increasing number of societies were actively acquiring books, correspondence, magazines, and newspapers for their own libraries. To a degree, these societies made Congress more aware of the national importance of both the science of agriculture and the American farmer. In 1852, the privately-supported United States Agricultural Society was formed based upon the principles originally laid down in Washington's last address to Congress.[100] At each of its annual meetings, the Society, along with the Maryland Agricultural Society and many other state and local groups, urged the establishment of a separate federally-funded entity. Finally, in 1862, some 66 years after Washington's recommendation, a national milestone in agriculture was achieved when Abraham Lincoln, another soft-spoken self-taught man, signed the Organic Act establishing the Department of Agriculture.[101]

More than any other figure of his time, Washington remained fully aware of "the importance of National encouragement to Agriculture."[102] He had been burdened as no other American leader of his era with the time-consuming challenges of completing the American Revolution and developing a viable national government. Yet, in the examination of his papers, the profile of George Washington that emerges reveals him as an agricultural agent for change. Washington pursued improvements in agriculture at his Mount Vernon estate, hoping to create an experimental showcase where his many visitors might witness new and more enlightened approaches to farming. Washington envisioned an agriculture based upon careful testing, a system of crop rotation which allowed profits to be maximized without ruining the soil, and a thoughtful integration of improved livestock as a long-term source of animal power, food, and fertilizer. During long periods away from home, there were times when Washington experienced setbacks and failures in his agricultural activities but he remained a persistent, innovative, and determined farmer until his final day. Whether involved in enhancing crops, farm technology, animal husbandry, or soil fertility, Washington's preoccupation with and love of farming at Mount Vernon was complemented by his national vision for the future of agriculture in the new America. His involvement in supporting the development of agricultural societies and his proposal for a National Board of Agriculture represented strong investments in the future, for Washington's ideas remained alive in the hearts of future generations of farmers.

Notes

1 Louis B. Wright, *The Cultural Life of the American Colonies, 1607-1763* (New York: Harper and Row, c1957, 1962), 2; John T. Schlebecker, *Whereby We Thrive: A History of American Farming, 1607-1972* (Ames, Iowa: Iowa State University Press, 1975), 37, 50; Aubrey C. Land, "A Modified Heritage: The Colonial Economy and Social Order as Seen in Literary and Non-Literary Sources" in *Agricultural Literature: Proud Heritage – Future Promise. . . ,* eds. Alan Fusonie and Leila Moran (Washington, D.C.: Associates of the National Agricultural Library, Inc. and the Graduate School Press, U.S. Department of Agriculture, 1977), 17; Clement Eaton, *A History of the Old South: The Emergence of a Reluctant Nation,* 3rd ed. (New York: Macmillan Publishing Co., 1975), 18.

2 Lois Green Carr and Lorena S . Walsh, "Economic Diversification and Labor Organization in the Chesapeake, 1650-1820," in *Work and Labor in Early America,* ed. Stephen Innes (Chapel Hill: University of North Carolina Press for The Institute of Early American History and Culture, 1988), 145, 151; Bruce A. Ragsdale, *A Planters' Republic: The Search for Economic Independence in Revolutionary Virginia* (Madison, Wisconsin: Madison House, 1996), 4, 8.

3 Wright, *Cultural Life,* 3-7, 15.

4 George Washington, *Journal of My Journey Over the Mountains, While Surveying for Lord Thomas Fairfax, Baron of Cameron, in the Northern Neck of Virginia Beyond the Blue Ridge, in 1747-8,* ed. J. M. Toner (Albany, New York: Joel Munsell's Sons, 1892), 10-11; Paul K. Longmore, *The Invention of George Washington* (Berkeley: University of California Press, c1988, 1989), 6-9; Ulrich Troubetzkoy, "George Washington, Surveyor," *Virginia Cavalcade,* 10, no. 3 (Winter 1960/61): 5-10.

5 John P. Riley, "Washington as Agricultural Revolutionary" (paper presented at the Society for Historians of the Early American Republic in Boston, July 15, 1994), 3, 5-6.

6 Riley, "Sobriety, Honesty, Industry: White Labor at Mount Vernon" (paper presented at the Northern Virginia Studies Conference, Northern Virginia Community College, November 5, 1992), 2-3; John C. Fitzpatrick, ed., *The Writings of George Washington,* 39 vols. (Washington, D.C.: United States Government Printing Office, 1931-1944), 37: 256-68 [hereafter cited as *Writings*].

7 Edmund S. Morgan, *The Meaning of Independence: John Adams, Thomas Jefferson, George Washington* (New York: W. W. Norton and Co., 1976), 30.

8 Bruce A. Ragsdale, "George Washington, the British Tobacco Trade, and Economic Opportunity in Prerevolutionary Virginia," in *Virginia*

Magazine of History and Biography, 97, no. 2 (April 1989): 137, 140-41, 143-44.

9   For a bibliography and partially annotated compilation of agricultural works acquired by GW, see *A Selected Bibliography on George Washington's Interest in Agriculture*, eds. Alan and Donna Jean Fusonie (Davis, California: Agricultural History Society, University of California, 1976); C. S. Orwin, *A History of English Farming* (London: Thomas Nelson and Sons, Ltd., 1949), 35, 52, 54; Donald Jackson and Dorothy Twohig, eds., *The Diaries of George Washington*, 6 vols. (Charlottesville: The University Press of Virginia, 1976-79), 1: xxviii, 260-61, 266-67, 275, 283 [hereafter cited as *Diaries*].

10   Ragsdale, "British Tobacco Trade," 138, 145, 147-48.

11   *Diaries*, 2:38; Paul Leland Haworth, *George Washington, Country Gentleman, Being An Account of His Home Life and Agricultural Activities* (Indianapolis: Bobbs-Merrill Co., 1925), 96-97.

12   *Diaries*, 2: 36, 43, 49-51, 56-57, 67, 70, 73-74, 76-77, 80-82, 90-92, 98-99, 105-6, 113.

13   Arthur Pierce Middleton, *Tobacco Coast, A Maritime History of the Chesapeake Bay in the Colonial Era* (Baltimore: Johns Hopkins University Press and the Maryland State Archives, c1958, 1994), 178-79.

14   *Writings*, 27: 224-25.

15   GW to Lafayette, 1 February 1784, in W. W. Abbot and Dorothy Twohig, *The Papers of George Washington, Confederation Series,* 6 vols. (Charlottesville: University Press of Virginia, 1992-1997), 1:88, [hereafter cited as *Papers, Confederation Series*]; GW to Adrienne, Marquise de Lafayette, 4 April 1784, in *Papers, Confederation Series,* 1:258.

16   GW to Fielding Lewis, Jr., 27 February 1784, in *Ibid*, 1:161.

17   See letters from GW to William Pearce, 24 May 1795, 25 October 1795, 3 April 1796, 8 May 1796, and 11 September 1796 in *Writings,* 34:203-206, 342-43; 35:9-12, 43-44, 206-207.

18   Presidential Papers Microfilm: George Washington Papers, Series 8A-D, Notes, Reel 124, Manuscripts Division, Library of Congress [hereafter cited as LCMD, GWP]; GW to Arthur Young, 6 August 1786, in *Papers, Confederation Series*, 4:196.

19   Arthur Young, "On the Conduct of Experiments in Agriculture," in *Annals of Agriculture and Other Useful Arts* (London, 1786), 5:24, 25.

20   GW to Arthur Young, 6 August 1786, in *Papers, Confederation Series*, 4:196.

21   Haworth, *Country Gentleman*, 116; *Diaries*, 1: xxviii-xxix; 5:207, 287.

22   *Diaries*, 5:125.

23   An examination of LCMD, GWP, Series 8A-D, Notes, Reel 124 reveals GW's careful sketching and notetaking from Henry Home's, *The*

Gentleman Farmer: Being An Attempt to Improve Agriculture by Subjecting It To The Test of Rational Principles (Edinburgh: Printed for W. Creech, 1776), pl. 1, 2; pp. 124, 129, 131.

24 John Beale Bordley, *A Summary View of the Courses of Crops, In The Husbandry of England and Maryland: With a Comparison of Their Products and a System of Improved Courses, Proposed for Farms in America* (Philadelphia: Charles Cist, 1784), [3]-22; Bordley, *Sketches on Rotations of Crops, and Other Rural Matters.* . . . (Philadelphia: Charles Cist, 1797), 1-38, 38-66; LCMD, GWP, 8A-D Notes, Reel 124; Bordley, *Essays and Notes on Husbandry and Rural Affairs* (Philadelphia: Budd and Bartram for Dobson, 1799), 5-7, 12-17. See also Ulysses P. Hedrick, *A History of Horticulture in America to 1860* (New York: Oxford University Press, 1950), 473.

25 GW to John Beale Bordley, 17 August 1788, in *Papers, Confederation Series,* 6:450.

26 *Diaries,* 5:302, 309. See also Carr and Walsh, "Economic Diversification," 178-79.

27 *Diaries,* 1:257.

28 GW to Theodorick Bland, 28 December 1786, in *Papers, Confederation Series,* 4:484.

29 GW to William Pearce, 6 October 1793, in *Writings,* 33:111.

30 GW to William Pearce, 25 January 1795, in *Writings,* 34:103.

31 Bordley, "Some Account of Treading Out Wheat," in *Sketch of the History of the Philadelphia Society for Promoting Agriculture,* 6 vols. (Philadelphia: Philadelphia Society for Promoting Agriculture, [1785], 1939), 6:115-121.

32 *Diaries,* 5:271-72; Jacques Jean Pierre Brissot de Warville, *New Travels in the United States of America Performed in 1788* (Dublin: W. Corbet, 1792), 428.

33 *Writings,* 33:132-133.

34 *Ibid,* 33:270.

35 *Ibid,* 33: 296; *Writings,* 34:193-94; Riley, "To Build a Barn," in *The Mount Vernon Ladies' Association* [hereafter MVLA] *Annual Report 1992* (Mount Vernon, VA: MVLA, 1992), 32-37.

36 *Writings,* 34:102.

37 *Diaries,* 6:313.

38 GW to George William Fairfax, 30 June 1785, in *Papers, Confederation Series,* 3:90.

39 *Writings,* 35:79; GW to Landon Carter, 17 October 1796, *Ibid,* 35:246.

40 Dennis J. Pogue, "Archaeological Investigations at the Dung Repository," in *The Annual Report of the Mount Vernon Ladies' Association 1993* (Mount Vernon, VA: MVLA, 1993), 27-31; GW to

William Pearce, 11 January 1795, *Writings*, 34:84; GW to Pearce, 10 May 1795, in *Ibid*, 35:193.

41 *Diaries*, 1:257-58.

42 Stevenson W. Fletcher, *Pennsylvania Agriculture and Country Life, 1640-1840* (Harrisburg: Pennsylvania Historical and Museum Commission, 1950), 198-200.

43 *Diaries*, 4:223-24, 228-30, 232-33, 239.

44 *Ibid*, 4:234; John Hervey et al., *Racing and Breeding in America and the Colonies* (London, England: The London and Counties Press Association, 1931), 3:12, 17.

45 *Diaries*, 1:243-45.

46 Donald Ransone Taylor, "The Sheep of Hog Island," in *American Minor Breeds Conservancy* (February 1986): 4; *The American Livestock Breeds Conservancy 1993 Breeders Directory* (Pittsboro, North Carolina: American Livestock Breeds Conservancy, 1993), 14; Livestock/Committee on Managing Global Genetic Resources: Agricultural Imperatives, Board on Agriculture, National Research Council, *Managing Global Livestock Genetic Resources* (Washington, D.C.: National Academy Press, 1993), 14-15; George W. P. Custis, *An Address to the People of the United States, On The Importance of Encouraging Agriculture and Domestic Manufactures . . . Together With An Account of The Improvement in Sheep at Arlington, The Native Sheep of Smith's Island, and the Plans Proposed of Extending This Valuable Race of Animals, For The Benefit of The Country at Large* (Alexandria, Virginia: Printed by S. Snowden, 1808); Cecil Gray, *History of Agriculture in the Southern United States to 1860* (Washington, D.C.: Carnegie Institute of Washington, 1933), 207-208.

47 Bordley, *Essays and Notes on Husbandry*, 176.

48 *Diaries*, 2:7, 13-14.

49 GW to William Fitzhugh, Jr., 15 May 1786, in *Papers, Confederation Series*, 4:52.

50 Young, *Annals*, 7:492.

51 GW to Arthur Young, 18 June 1792, in *Writings*, 32:70.

52 GW to Sir John Sinclair, 20 July 1794, in *Writings*, 33:439.

53 *Diaries*, 5:469; John Beale Bordley, *Purport of a Letter on Sheep Written in Maryland, March 30th, 1789* (Philadelphia, 1789), 1.

54 Samuel Deane, *The New England Farmer. . .* (Worcester, MA: Isaik Thomas, 1790), 246. "Summary of Facts Relative to American Sheep ... Transmitted to the English Board of Agriculture by General Washington, in 1794," in *The Agricultural Museum: . . . A Repository of Valuable Information To The Farmer and Manufacturer.* (Georgetown: W. A. Rind, 1811), 143.

55 GW to Arthur Young, 18-21 June 1792, in *Writings*, 32:70; GW to

William Pearce, 9 February 1794, in *Ibid*, 33:278-79.

56 GW to William Pearce, 6 April 1794, in *Writings*, 33:316-17. Note that around this time, Washington acquired the work of Peter Simon Pallas, *An Account of the Different Kinds of Sheep Found in the Russian Dominions and Among the Tartar Horses of Asia* (Edinburgh, 1794).

57 *Diaries*, 1:343.

58 Herman R. Purdy and R. John Daws, *Breeds of Cattle* (New York, NY: Chanticleer Press, 1987), 179; *Transactions of the Franklin County Agricultural Society* (Greenfield, Massachusetts, 1892), 9-10; Rodolphus Dickenson, *Geographical and Statistical View of Massachusetts Proper* (Greenfield, Massachusetts, 1818), 7, 12; Gray, *History of Agriculture*, 204.

59 *Diaries*, 1:xxxiv, 268; *Ibid*, 5:311; GW to William Pearce, 9 February 1794, in *Writings*, 33:267; GW to James Anderson, in *Writings*, 37:462.

60 *Diaries*, 4:249.

61 GW to William Pearce, 23 November 1794, in *Writings*, 34:43.

62 Brissot de Warville, *New Travels*, 428. His account of the Mount Vernon visit is reprinted in Arthur Young, *Annals*, 18:158-59; *Diaries*, 4:104, 274; 5:72.

63 GW to Robert Townsend Hooe, [18 July 1784], in *Papers, Confederation Series*, 2:2; Thomas Jefferson to GW, 10 December 1784, in *Ibid*, 2:176-77; *Diaries*, 4:213-14.

64 GW to John Fairfax, 26 October 1785, in *Papers, Confederation Series*, 3:320-22; GW to Francisco Rendon, 19 December 1785, *Ibid*, 3:473-75; GW to Bushrod Washington, 13 April 1786, *Ibid*, 4:18; GW to Robert Townsend Hooe, 18 July 1784, *Ibid*, 2:2; GW to Bushrod Washington, 13 April 1786, *Ibid*, 4:18; GW to William Fitzhugh, Jr., 5 June 1786, *Ibid*, 4:94.

65 Lafayette to GW, 7 February 1787, in *Papers, Confederation Series*, 5:13-14; GW to Arthur Young, 4 December 1788, in W. W. Abbot and Dorothy Twohig, eds., *The Papers of George Washington, Presidential Series*, 6 vols. to date (Charlottesville: University Press of Virginia, 1987-), 1:160-61.

66 *Diaries*, 4:239; W. K. Bixby, ed., *Inventory of the Contents of Mount Vernon, 1810* (Cambridge U.S.A.: University Press, 1909), 50-57.

67 John Stuart Skinner, "The Ass and the Mule" in *The Horse*, ed. William Youatt (Philadelphia: Porter Coats, 1843), 423.

68 *Diaries*, 1:264-65.

69 *Ibid*, 3:7, 46.

70 *Diaries*, 3:24.

71 G. Terry Sharrer, "Flour Milling in the Growth of Baltimore, 1750-1830," *Maryland Historical Magazine* 71 (Fall, 1976): 329; Stuart

Bruchey, *Growth of Modern American Economy* (New York: Dodd, Mead and Co., 1975), 65.

72 GW's Ledger B: Folio 333, copy in Collections of MVLA.

73 GW to William Pearce, 7 February 1796, in *Writings*, 34:449; GW to Pearce, 2 November 1794, *Writings*, 34:14; GW to Pearce, 23 November 1794, *Writings*, 34:43; GW to Pearce, 30 November 1794, *Writings*, 34:48.

74 Douglas C. North, *The Economic Growth of the United States, 1790-1860* (New York: W. W. Norton and Company, 1966), 19; *Diaries*, 3:36, 37, 120.

75 GW to William Pearce, 6 April 1794, in *Writings*, 33:314-15.

76 Ragsdale, "British Tobacco Trade," 143-44; GW to William Pearce, 31 August 1794, in *Writings*, 33:490.

77 GW to James Anderson, 15 January 1797, Washington MSS, MVLA.

78 James Anderson to GW, 21 June 1797, copy in Washington MSS, MVLA; GW to James Anderson, 6 February 1798, in *Writings*, 36:153-54.

79 GW to Samuel Davidson, 2 March 1798, in *Writings*, 36:177.

80 GW to William Augustine Washington, 5 April 1798, in *Writings*, 36:240; GW to William Augustine Washington, 26 June 1798, in *Writings*, 36:302-303.

81 GW to James Anderson, 16 September 1798, Washington MSS, MVLA.

82 Julian Ursyn Niemcewicz, *Under Their Vine and Fig Tree: Travels through America in 1797-1799, 1805, . . .* trans. and ed. Metchie J. E. Budka (Elizabeth, N.J.: The Grassmann Publishing Co., 1965), 100.

83 James Anderson to GW, 22 February 1797, copy in Washington MSS, MVLA; Mount Vernon Farm Ledger, 1798-1801, Folio 46, Washington MSS, MVLA; Mount Vernon Farm Ledger, 1797-1798, copy in Washington MSS, MVLA, Folio 87, indicates that in its first year of operation, the distillery was listed as the third most profitable business enterprise after milling and the fisheries.

84 *Diaries*, 1:214-15.

85 GW to Arthur Young, 12 December 1793, in *Writings*, 33:176.

86 *Diaries*, 1:261; 2:165.

87 *Diaries*, 4:329.

88 *Ibid*, 2:272; 3:240-41.

89 Donald McDonald, *Agricultural Writers from Sir Walter of Henley to Arthur Young, 1200-1800* (London: n.p., 1908), 4; Rodney True, "Sketch of the History of the Philadelphia Society for Promoting Agriculture," *Memoirs of the Philadelphia Society for Promoting Agriculture*, 6 vols. (Philadelphia: Philadelphia Society for Promoting Agriculture, 1939), 6:5; *New York Gazette*, 13 March 1766; *New York Mercury*, 10 March 1766; *Weekly Post Boy*, 13 March 1766; *American*

Husbandry, Containing an Account of the Soil, Climate, Production and Agriculture of the British Colonies in North America and the West Indies; . . . (London: J. Bew, 1775), 1:180.

90   *An Address from the Philadelphia Society for Promoting Agriculture; . . .* (Philadelphia: The Philadelphia Society for Promoting Agriculture, 1785), A2; Minutes Book of the Philadelphia Society for Promoting Agriculture, 1787-1810 (unpublished manuscript), 60; *Diaries,* 5:173.

91   *Laws of the Philadelphia Society for Promoting Agriculture; . . .* (Philadelphia: The Philadelphia Society for Promoting Agriculture, 1787), 3-9.

92   Richard Peters, *Agricultural Enquiries on Plaister of Paris. . . .* (Philadelphia: Charles Cist and John Markland, 1797), iii-iv; *American Museum* 9 (January 1791): 41-44, 109-11; GW to Richard Peters, 21 January 1787, in *Writings,* 35:371.

93   See *The Pennsylvania Mercury,* 14 September 1787, for a descriptive account of an on-site observation of the Hessian Fly on Long Island; Bordley, *Essays and Notes,* 242; Wayne D. Rasmussen, "The Farmer in the Evolution of a New Nation, 1763-1788," (June 27, 1960), 11 [mimeographed copy courtesy of the author].

94   GW to James Warren, 7 October 1785, in *Papers, Confederation Series,* 3:300.

95   GW to Drayton, *Papers, Confederation Series,* 3:605-06.

96   GW to Newenham, 29 August 1788, in *Papers, Confederation Series,* 6:487; GW to Lafayette, 18 June 1788, in *Ibid,* 6:338.

97   GW to Young, 5 December 1791, in *Writings,* 31:440.

98   GW to Sinclair, 20 July 1794, in *Writings,* 33:438.

99   Eighth Annual Address to Congress, in *Writings,* 35:315-16; GW to Sinclair, 10 December 1796, in *Writings,* 35:321-23.

100 *The Journal of Agriculture: Comprising the Transactions and the Correspondence of the United States Agricultural Society,* 3 (April 1860): 161. For a selective list of monographs, periodicals, and works of agricultural societies published prior to 1860 see *Heritage of American Agriculture: A Bibliography of pre-1860 Imprints* (Beltsville, MD: National Agricultural Library, United States Department of Agriculture, 1975), Library List 98, compiled by Alan M. Fusonie.

101 Alan Fusonie, "History of the National Agricultural Library," *Agricultural History,* 62, no.2 (Spring 1988): 189-207.

102 GW to Sir John Sinclair, 20 January 1799, in *Writings,* 36:97.

About the Authors

Alan and Donna Jean Fusonie received their B.A. degrees from Lenoir Rhyne College and Hollins College, respectively, and advanced degrees from Catholic University of America. Both worked for a number of years at the Department of Agriculture, Alan as Head of Special Collections at the National Agricultural Library and Donna Jean as Director of the Reference Center at the Economic Research Service. Alan has also taught American history in Maryland at Prince Georges' Community College and Charles County Community College. Donna Jean is completing her first children's book.

As researchers and editors, their past publication experience includes bibliographies, articles, and books relating to early American agriculture. They live on a farm in Vermont where they pursue their agricultural and research interests.